THE BEEKEEPERS ANNUAL
IS PUBLISHED BY
NORTHERN BEE BOOKS
MYTHOLMROYD, WEST YORKSHIRE
& PRINTED BY
LIGHTNING SOURCE, UK
ISBN 978-1-904846-34-5

MMVIII

EDITOR, JOHN PHIPPS
NEOCHORI, 24024 AGIOS NIKOLAOS,
MESSINIAS, GREECE
EMAIL manifest@runbox.com

SET IN HELVETICA LT BY D&P Design and Print

Front Cover
Honeybee about to visit a sunflower -
but how much poison lies unseen within
its nectaries? *by John Phipps*

CONTENTS

FOREWORD

John Phipps

September 2009

2008 will undoubtedly be remembered as a year of extreme optimism in the beekeeping community. Despite winter losses of bees of up to 30%, the number of new recruits to the craft has risen by the same percentage. It seems that many people have taken to heart the prediction that without bees the planet would be doomed, a message often repeated by the media when reporting on the unexplained colony losses, not only in the UK, but globally too. Membership of beekeeping associations has increased to the point where there is a waiting list for course attendance - as well as a shortage of bees to fill the hives of beginners. At the same time, there has been a drive to show that beekeeping is not just a rural pursuit but a hobby suitable for the urban or city dweller, too (and if a garden isn't available, a roof top will do), with promises of high honey yields; indeed, London roof top honey is selling currently at £10 per half a pound. Not surprisingly, some interest was shown recently in a new hive, purposely designed for the city dweller, selling for £500. One hopes that the great enthusiasm being shown at present is sustained, for it takes a lot of knowledge and experience for a beekeeper just to keep bees alive at this difficult time, let alone being able to produce a good crop of honey.

The photographs prefacing each of the months in the calendar section of this annual are taken from the covers of various past issues of The Beekeepers Quarterly, which reaches its 100th edition in May 2010. It is our intention to produce a special 100th issue which we plan to have ready for the BBKA Stoneleigh Convention in April. The Beekeepers Quarterly came into being, initially, as a means of updating the Annual, the first two issues carrying the title 'The Supplement'. It is from that eight-page black and white publication that The Beekeepers Quarterly has developed into a sixty-page full-colour

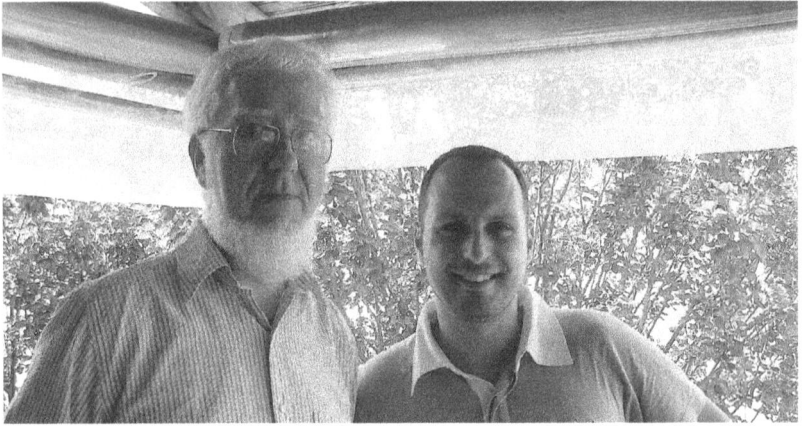

JOHN PHIPPS WITH SPIROS SKAREAS, WHO WORKS AS AN ADVISOR FOR THE LARGEST GREEK HONEY PACKAGING PLANT, ATTIKI-PITTAS.

journal - the first beekeeping magazine in the UK to be in the A4 format which has now also been adopted by other UK beekeeping magazines.

In this publication we have a small quote from 'The Times Beemaster' who advocated simplicity in beekeeping. There are many gimmicks and gimmicky ways of keeping bees, but the really important things are to let the bees live as natural a life as possible, interfere with them as little as possible and ensure that their health and nutrional needs are met at the right time.

John Phipps
September 2009

4th COLLOSS CONFERENCE, Prevention of honeybee COony LOSses

●

This pan global meeting of scientists from 24 countries took place in Zagreb from the 3rd-4th March, 2009. Each of the representatives was given the opportunity of giving statistics for the colony losses in their own country as well as suggesting the possible causes of mortality. The meeting was prefaced with a brief history of CCD and its most likely symptoms by Jamie D Ellis of the Honey Bee Research and Extension Laboratory, University of Florida:

Colony Collapse Disorder (CCD) was first noted in the U.S. in fall 2006. At that time, some beekeepers living in states reporting CCD lost 30-90% of their colonies when 10-20% losses were considered normal. The Apiary Inspectors of America and USDA-ARS estimate that honey bee colony losses for fall/winter 2006-2007 and 2007-2008 were 31% and 36% respectively. These loss estimates are based on phone surveys of beekeepers who manage between 10-18% of the 2.4 million colonies in the U.S. Numerous causes, including CCD, were reported as contributing to the colony losses in both 2007 and 2008. In an attempt to remove the ambiguity surrounding CCD, U.S. bee scientists defined the symptoms associated with the phenomenon. In collapsed colonies, CCD may produce the following symptoms: (1) the complete absence of adult bees in colonies with few or no dead bees in/around colonies, (2) the presence of capped brood, and (3) the presence of food stores that are not robbed by other bees or typical colony pests. CCD symptoms associated with collapsing (weakening) colonies include: (1) an insufficient number of bees to maintain the amount of brood in the colony, (2) the workforce is composed largely of younger adult bees, (3) the queen is present, and (4) the cluster of bees is reluctant to consume food provided to them by the beekeeper. The cause(s) of CCD in U.S. bee colonies remains under investigation. Currently, many conceivable and realistic hypotheses remain plausible. Not listed in any particular order, these hypotheses include, but are not limited to: (1) traditional bee pests and diseases, (2) how the bees were managed, (3) queen source (poor genetic biodiversity), (4) chemical use in bee colonies, (5) chemical toxins in the environment, (6) varroa mites and associated pathogens, (7) bee nutritional fitness, (8) undiscovered/newly-discovered pests and pathogens, and (9) potential synergistic interactions between two or more of the hypotheses. Other hypotheses have been proposed (genetically modified crops, climate change, etc.) but those listed above currently are the most investigated. Considerable funding for CCD research has become available in the U.S. and progress has been achieved on many collaborative research fronts. These include studying the effects of pesticides on bees, understanding the biology of new pests/pathogens, recognizing the effects of environmental and management stresses on bees, etc. In general, there are two large CCD research efforts in the U.S., the first being the USDA Area-Wide project and the second being the BEE CAP project. In addition to these well-funded efforts, many bee scientists in the U.S. have formed partnerships with colleagues nationally and internationally, creating a well-defined, collaborative colony loss research effort.

The report for the UK was prepared by Selwyn Wilkins, Gay Marris, Giles Budge and Mike Brown, of the Food and Environment Research Agency, formerly the Central Science Laboratory, National Bee Unit.

Honey bee colony losses in the United Kingdom
Honey bees are vital pollinators in commercial crop production (estimated UK value £200 m.p.a.), and also in natural ecosystems, where their role in maintaining biodiversity is almost incalculable. The value of UK honey production varies between £10 to £35 m.p.a. It is estimated that there are 230,000 colonies in England, managed by ~30,000 beekeepers, of which 99% are hobbyist, and only 1% commercial enterprise; Wales has ~20,000 colonies and 4,000 beekeepers; Scotland has ~36,000 colonies and 6,000 beekeepers; in Northern Ireland 4,000 colonies are managed by 1,000 beekeepers. Recently, beekeepers across North America and Europe have reported increased and sudden losses of colonies. The term colony collapse disorder (CCD) has been used to describe this phenomenon in

Table 1: Overview of colony losses in the participating countries based on data presented in the submitted abstracts. The number of beekeepers and colonies, year of survey, colony losses [%], N = sample size of checked colonies, type of survey, presence of *Nosema ceranae* and iAPV (unknown=?) and references are given (author and page number in the Proceedings of the 4th COLOSS Conference).

Country	Beekeepers	Colonies	Years	Losses [%]	N	Type of survey	N. ceranae	iAPV	Author(s), page(s)
Austria	22198	278810	2007/08	13.3	16217	questionnaire	YES	NO	Craisheim et al. p. 7
Belgium	8600	101600	2004/05, 2006/07	16.4, 7.3		questionnaire, visits, sampling	?	?	Nguyen et al., p. 8
Bulgaria	40000	750000	2006/07, 2007/08	6, 10	13000	phone survey	?	?	Ivanova & Petrov. p. 10
Croatia			2008/09	15.3	10293	questionnaire	YES	?	Kezić et al. p. 12
Denmark	4100		2007/08	32	17000	questionnaire	YES	NO	Vejsnæs & Kryger. p. 13
Finland	2700	53000	2007/08	16	3514	voluntary survey	YES	NO	Korpela et al. p. 16
France	69000	1300000	2007/08	15, 29.3	2826, 62400	random survey; CNDA survey	YES	YES	Chauzat et al. p. 17
Germany	85000	900000	2004ff	8-16	7200	DEBIMO	YES	YES	Büchler et al. p. 19
Greece	22000	1300000	2006/07, 2007/08	15, 14	26000, 48250	questionnaire	YES	?	Hatjina et al., p. 21
Hungary	15000	800000	2007/08	10-30	170	Diagnostic program	YES	NO	Békési & Matray, p. 22
Ireland	2000	20000	2006/07, 2008/09	53, 15-20	891	questionnaire; unofficial estimates	YES		Coffey & Breen. p. 23
Israel	450	100000	2008/09	20	46000	questionnaire	YES	YES	Soroker et al. p. 24
Italy	75000	1157133	2007/08	37.4	5973	questionnaire	YES	NO	Mutinelli et al. p. 26
Former Yugoslav Republic of Macedonia	10000	75000		18	11912	questionnaire	NO	NO	Uzunov et al., p. 29
Netherlands	8000		2007/08	23	7434	NCB Dutch monitor	YES	NO	Blacquière & van der Zee, p. 30
Norway	3000	60000	2007/08	10.1	17872	questionnaire	YES	NO	Dahle, p. 32
Poland	40000	1000000	2007/08	15.3	26710	questionnaire	YES	?	Topolska et al. p. 33
Portugal	15000	550000	2006	30.3		national survey	?	?	Murilhas, p. 35
Serbia	20000	400000	2007/08	27.5		estimation	YES	NO	Mladenović et al. p. 36
Slovenia	8000	170000	2007/08	30-50	33890	estimation of total population	YES	?	Gregorc & Kralj, p. 38
Sweden	12000	125000	2006/07, 2007/08	12, 17	31400	questionnaire	YES	?	Kristiansen & Fries, p. 40
Switzerland	18000	190000	2002/03, 2006/07	23, 18	8200, 35000	questionnaire; monitoring system survey	YES	?	Charrière & Neumann, p. 41
Turkey	33770	3300000	2006/07, 2007/08	30, 1.8		questionnaire	YES	?	Ozkurim et al., p. 42
United Kingdom	41000	290000	2007/08	33	10897	questionnaire	YES	NO	Wilkins et al., p. 43
USA		2400000	2006/07, 2007/08	31, 36		Apiary Inspectors America/USDA-ARS	YES	YES	Ellis et al., p. 45

the US. However, the specific symptoms associated with CCD have not been described in the UK where, historically, annual colony losses have fluctuated greatly. Since 2001, when pyrethroid resistant Varroa mites were first detected, there has been a gradual increase in colony losses in the UK. In 2008, Winter/Spring losses for England and Wales, based on the results of a survey of 1,385 beekeepers owning 10,897 colonies, showed over-winter losses of 33% for 2008. Total losses throughout 2008 were 12% (26,463 colonies inspected). Over-winter losses in Scotland for 2008 based on a Scottish Beekeeping Association written survey of 10% of it's membership were 27%. Anecdotal evidence for Northern Ireland suggests that colony losses for the same period were >20%. The major impact on colony survival across the UK has been the Varroa mite, but other pathogens, pesticides, bee nutrition and colony management by the beekeeper have also been implicated. It is likely that the increased honey bee mortality may not be due to a single factor, but to multi-factorial interactions between these various stressors. In England and Wales a Bee Health Strategy has been developed by The Department for Environment and Rural Affairs (Defra) and The Welsh Assembly Government (WAG), in conjunction with key industry Stakeholders. This sets out a plan for the future direction of work aimed at sustaining the health of honey bees and beekeeping in England and Wales for the next decade (Parallel programmes are being considered in Scotland and Northern Ireland). It sets out five key outcomes: 1) Effective communications and relationships operate at all levels; 2) Effective biosecurity minimises risks from pests, diseases and undesirable species; 3) Good standards of beekeeping and husbandry minimise pest and disease risks and contribute to sustaining honey bee populations – prevention is better than cure; 4) Impacts from pests, diseases and other hazards are kept to the lowest levels practicable; and, 5) Sound science and evidence underpins bee health policy and its implementation. The strategy proposes objectives and activities that will contribute to achieving these desired outcomes. The National Bee Unit will be instrumental in the implementation of the strategy. Information gathered through the work of the strategy can be used to feed into the European COLLOSS working group.

COLLOSS, the network of researchers studying colony loss in 36 countries, is organised by Peter Neumann of the Swiss Bee Research Centre in Berne.

PESTICIDES AND THE ENVIRONMENT - with special reference to the Neonicotinoids

On the 8th September an important research paper was delivered to Michael Jacobs, the Prime Minister's Special Advisor on Environmental Issues at a bee summit at 10 Downing Street. The report, initiated by BUGLIFE, 'The impact of neonicotionoid insecticides on bumblebees, Honeybees and other non target invertebrates', by Vicky Kindemba, reviews existing approvals research and independent research on these new pesticides. In brief:

'the findings reveal a disparity between independent research and the research that was undertaken by Bayer, the producer of the neonicotinoid pesticide imidacloprid, for the imidacloprid 'Draft Assessment Report' (DAR), the 2005 report that was the foundation of the EU regulatory approvals process for this pesticide. Independent research found significant negative impacts on bees that were not included in the DAR because the research was invalidated by the DAR. The basis for this invalidation is questionable, but it resulted in key evidence not being considered as part of the approvals process.'

Buglife, the Soil Association, Pesticides Action Network and Bumblebee Conservation Trust are therefore calling for the suspension of all UK approvals for products containing neonicotinoids that are used outdoors and a review of all neonicotinoid approvals. In addition they are demanding that more comprehensive methodologies for assessing the effects pesticides on non-target invertebrates are incorporated into approval procedures.

The whole of this report can be viewed on-line, or downloaded, by going on to Buglife's website, (Just google 'Buglife').

Included in the appendix of the report is the letter sent to the EU at the beginning of this year by the Belgian Director of Nature and Honey, which is reproduced here in full.

AANTEKENEN
Androulla Vassiliou
European Commissioner for Health
DG Health and Consumer protection
B-1049 Brussels
Belgium
Utrecht, 21 Januari 2009
our reference: HM/jc/090120.01-4.1.0.40.N08
contact: Mr. H. Muilerman
subject: Re: Request for an internal review of Commission Regulation 116/2008

Dear Commissioner,
I am writing on behalf of undersigned organisations to submit a formal request for an internal review (based on Regulation 1367/2006, article 10) of Commission Directive 116/2008 of 15/12/2008 which was published in the Official Journal of 16/12/2008. It is the opinion of our organisations that Commission Directive 116/2008, including the active substance Imidacloprid in Annex I of Directive 91/414, is not justified on several grounds and should be reviewed as a matter of urgency. Please find below the basis of our request.

Procedural criteria:
Our organisations are entitled to make this request because we fulfil the criteria laid down in article 11 of Regulation 1367/2006. Stichting Natuur en Milieu, PAN-Europe, Inter Environnement Wallonie, Nature et Progres and MDRGF France are all independent non-profit- making legal persons in accordance with the national law. Promoting environmental protection is one of our central objectives which we are actively pursuing.

Grounds for internal review:

Article 5 of Directive 91/414 on the inclusion of active substances in Annex I requires that active substances are expected to fulfil the condition of having no unacceptable influence on the environment as provided for in Article 4.1.b. IV and V (the article which is the basis for member states authorising the use of formulations based on the active substance). In our opinion however, the evidence presented by the Commission does not support the conclusion that the effects of the use of Imidacloprid on bees are acceptable.

EFSA concludes in its peer review of 29/5/2008 that spraying of imidacloprid (and its two main metabolites) poses a high risk to bees. The report recommends risk mitigation measures (no application during flowering, flowering weeds are removed) but concludes that bees will still be not protected by the suggested risk mitigation measures. For tomato production, for example, the situation is even more acute, as the EFSA peer review states, because tomatoes are flowering all the time. In relation to all spraying applications it is clear that the Commission has not demonstrated that acceptable use is possible.

Regarding the use of imidacloprid as a seed coating we think the tests performed by the notifier are inadequate in relation to bees and more generally to other pollinators. Below we present further arguments and comment relating to the DAR by the Rapporteur Germany.

Annex VI of Directive 91/414 (Uniform principles) on testing determines in 2.5.2.3.: Where there is a possibility of honeybees being exposed, no authorization shall be granted if the hazard quotients for oral or contact exposure of honeybees are greater than 50, unless it is clearly established through an appropriate risk assessment that under field conditions there are no unacceptable effects on honeybee larvae, honeybee behaviour, or colony survival and development after use of the plant protection product according to the proposed conditions of use.

Imidacloprid is simultaneously persistent, systemic, and highly toxic for bees (LD50 at 48 hours is 4.8 ppb (part per billion). Used in seed coatings, Imidacloprid is absorbed by the root system and transported by sap to all parts of the plant, including nectar and pollen. As the active substance is present in soil, even succeeding crops absorb residues and become toxic (cf. Annex B.9. p. 919 and following, and several scientific papers[1]).

1) Because contaminated nectar and pollen may be brought to the hive by the foragers, all the bees classes (drones, queens, nurses, larvae etc.) are potentially exposed to the active substance. The sensitivity of bees is now well understood and differs according to their class[2]. The necessary tests specific to each bee class have not been carried out. The closest estimates available document chronic toxicity (P. 965) in 'young bees' and 'old bees'.

They show a difference of sensitivity between these two categories of bee.

2) Another important point is that no bee brood feeding test has been carried out (point B.9.4.2., p. 926). Following the report: 'it has to be expected that the active substance and the formulated compounds are as toxic to larvae as to adult bees'. There is absolutely no scientific argument to support this assertion. The toxicity of a pesticide to one category of bees cannot be deduced from its toxicity to another; some substances are more toxic to larvae than to adult bees and vice versa3. Moreover, we recall the statement of the French State Council suspending the Maize authorization of Gaucho, based on the absence of this test despite the very high HQ (Hazard Quotient) value of Imidacloprid (40 540; cf. Reasoned statement of the overall conclusion, p. 57). Authorizing Imidacloprid without carrying out the larvae test is a clear violation of Directive 91/414 and unacceptable from a scientific viewpoint, as the innocuousness for larvae is not proved. If the European Authority estimates that the HQ is not a valid concept for seed coatings, a new assessment scheme has to be described before to assess the concerned substance, and included in annex VI of the 91/414/EEC Directive. Until then, the clauses in Annex VI, point B and C 2.5.2.3 must fully be enforced. The HQ (or TER: Toxicity Exposure Ratio) concepts have been designed to avoid making higher tier tests with low risk substances. In no case the arbitrary choice of discarding the HQ (this HQ validity not being investigated so far) for seed coating substances can be used to lower the risk. Consequently all the prescribed tests should be realized. Moreover, Imidacloprid is also formulated for spraying (e.g. Confidor). From a legal point of view, the lack of bee brood feeding test is thus sufficient to definitely invalidate the assessment that the HQ is not relevant in this case.

3) The report does not include any test about the effects of contaminated pollen consumption during wintering. The amount of pollen consumed by winter bees is unknown at this time. Every beekeeper knows that wintering may succeed only if the bee colony has collected important quantities of pollen during summer. Most of this pollen will disappear during winter and early spring: it has been consumed by the bees, and particularly by the nurses for feeding the early brood. The winter bees are not numerous (5,000-10,000) and, as they live much longer then summer bees, they will feed brood for a long period. This means that pollen consumption per winter bee may be very important compared to summer bees. Thus the pollen toxicity for winter bees has to be tested specifically. Before carrying out this test, it is necessary to quantify the pollen amounts consumed by winter bees with great care in order to define their exposure.

4) The dossier includes a point about chronic mortality, examining the LD50c of Imidacloprid and several metabolites. This point doesn't allow to conclude to Imidacloprid innocuousness for reasons as follows:

a) Data are provided for two metabolites only (urea and 6-chloronicotinic acid). No values are provided for olefin and 5-hydroxy-imidacloprid when these metabolites are hazardous for bees (they have a low acute LD50) and are detected in pollen and nectar. The explanation of this choice (point B.9.4.7.4.1 p. 962) is not credible: it is based on a scientific article (Suchail et al. 2001) that in contrary shows the significant lethal toxicity of olefin and 5-hydroxy-imidalcoprid.

b) The study (Suchail et al. 2001) shows firstly that the chronic toxicity is significantly higher than the acute toxicity, and secondly that for most of the metabolites, the mortality is the same for all the tested concentrations including very low concentrations (0.1ppb, more or less 0.1 ng/bee). This study is invalidated in the DAR (p. 961 sq), based on its discrepancy with other studies of the scientific literature. We cannot agree with this argument because:

i) the study (Suchail et al. 2001) tests substances amounts and concentrations that are significantly lower than the other studies and concludes to an equal substance toxicity for all the low concentration for most of the metabolites; if these other studies didn't test such low concentration, it is logical that they only detect higher LD50c.

ii) the study (Suchail et al. 2001) is published and peer-reviewed; moreover, it was validated by the French Comité scientifique et technique, based on the validity criteria elaborated by this Comité for analysing the existing literature4. The DAR considers it non-valid by comparison with LD50c measured in other studies, without verifying these other studies validity, what is not admissible from a scientific point of view.

iii) An Imidacloprid characteristic is the great variance shown by the mortality measurements, acute as well as chronic. For instance (Suchail et al. 2001) itself concludes to a acute toxicity of 57 ± 28 ng/bee, that to say to an acute LD50 significantly higher than the figure finally considered by the DAR (4,8 ng/bee). As a consequence a study cannot be invalidated on the single reason that the measured lethal toxicity figure departs from those found in other studies, without further verification.

5) The substance is neurotoxic and can have sub-lethal effects, making the bee unable to perform all its behavioural schemes, which are necessary for the colony survival. The report estimates that the NOEL (No Observed Effect Level) is 1.2 ng per bee, leading to a non-effect concentration of 46 ppb

(point B.9.4.7.3.1, p. 959). This figure is incorrect because it is based on a consumption of 20 µl per bee, corresponding to the syrup amount given to each bee following the DL50 test design. In reality a bee consumes much more nectar than that. Rortais et al (2005)5 estimate the forager consumption to be between 224 and 898.8 mg in seven days. We can make a quick estimation: a colony harvests 60 kg of honey, that is to say 150 kg nectar during one month (an average during the sunflower blossom). Two foragers generation must be considered, or about 20,000 foragers (it is commonly considered that a hive has about 10,000 foragers simultaneously). In his life, each bee will harvest 7.5 g of nectar from which about 10 % is used for the forager itself. So each bee will ingest about 750 mg in 2 weeks, or 107 mg in 48 hours. The other part of nectar is brought to the hive, but is in contact with the oesophagus and the stomach of the bee and so can have a contact toxicity. So the calculated NOEC in real conditions should be at least 10 times lower than the value estimated in the report. The real calculated NOEC should be below 5 ppb.

6) The DAR quotes the study (Guez et al. 2001) that shows significant sub-lethal effects on bees for concentrations between 0.1 and 10ppb. This study is also peer-reviewed. However, the DAR (p. 960) turns down this study conclusion on the grounds that the bees were reared in an incubator and subjected to an ice narcosis, and that these practices are suspected to modify bees learning abilities. This argument ignores the fact that the authors have observed the sub-lethal effects by comparison between a treated sample and a control sample that was subjected to the same rearing and narcosis; thus the argument is inadmissible and the study may not be dismissed.

7) None of the field and tunnel tests submitted in the report proves that the treated pollen has really been consumed during the test. Pollen consumption is always postponed by the bees as pollen needs a lactic fermentation during at least 10 days to be digested, and may remain several months in the combs cells. During all tests, the hives are put in the tunnel or fields contain feed combs. The submitted tests don't take this fact into account; they don't prove that the bees consume the contaminated food rather than the comb food; since it is more likely they use first the comb feed. Thus the tests conclude on the absence of effects while the real exposition is not proved. This is scientifically unacceptable.

8) Several tests leave us in doubt. For example, it is impossible to assess the queen eggs-laying in a small colony of 500 bees, as described in several tests, particularly in cage tests (point B.9.4.4). The queen eggs-laying depends on the number of nurses able to take care of the larvae. A normal queen lays 1000 to 1500 eggs per day, assuming a colony of more than 50

000 bees, that's to say 100 times more than the small colonies used in the tests. So the really eggs-laying cannot be fully assessed in so small colonies. Moreover the small colonies are unable to develop all the behaviours needed by the survival of a normal colony (e.g. developing a drone population, vitality, sufficient cells production…).

9) All these concerns are closely linked to the irrelevance of the current assessment scheme for systemic insecticides since they are susceptible to remain in contact with bees during long period of time because they potentially contaminate the foraged matrices: pollen and honey stocks. The scheme irrelevance has been emphasized by scientific papers[6] and is currently widely accepted. This definitely invalidates the global assessment process. Scientists admit today a PEC/PNEC (Predicted Environmental Concentration / Predicted No Effect Concentration) approach to be more relevant to assess the risk for bees of systemic, neurotoxic and persistent active substances or plant protection products (PPP). Halm et al (2006) and the French Comité Scientifique et Technique (CST) have tried this approach[7]; both of this papers conclude on the fact that the Imidacloprid PEC/PNEC ratio is alarming.

We quote here the CST conclusions:
(1) Dans l'état actuel de nos connaissances, selon les scénarios développés pour évaluer l'exposition et selon les facteurs d'incertitude choisis pour évaluer les dangers, les rapports PEC/PNEC obtenus sont préoccupants. Ils sont en accord avec les observations de terrain rapportées par de nombreux apiculteurs en zones de grande culture (maïs, tournesol), concernant la mortalité des butineuses (scénario 4), leur disparition, leurs troubles comportementaux et certaines mortalités d'hiver (scénario 5). En conséquence, l'enrobage de semences de tournesol Gaucho® conduit à un risque significatif pour les abeilles de différents âges, à l'exception des butineuses lorsqu'elles ingèrent du pollen lors de la confection de pelotes (scénario 3). En ce qui concerne l'enrobage Gaucho® de semences de maïs, le rapport PEC/PNEC s'avère, comme pour le tournesol, préoccupant dans le cadre de la consommation de pollen par les nourrices, ce qui pourrait entraîner une mortalité accrue de celles–ci et être un des éléments de l'explication de l'affaiblissement des populations d'abeilles encore observé malgré l'interdiction du Gaucho® sur tournesol.

10) The sowing dust effects are not assessed in the report. It is however a very important way of contamination, already scientifically studied in Italy[8]. Recently high bees mortalities occurred in Italy (Padanian plain, during spring 2007 and 2008) and Germany (Land of Baden-Württemberg during spring 2008). The DAR's conclusions about the risk for bees (Reasoned statement of the overall conclusion, p. 58) are entirely based on the postulate that

the bee exposure doesn't exceed a 5 ppb concentration. This postulate appears illusive. Investigating hives damages in the Lombardian plain (spring 2008), the Servizio Veterinario della Lombardia have found up to 144 ppb of Imidacloprid in bees. A single pollen sample was analyzed, giving the amazing Imidacloprid concentration of 311 ppb. During the Baden-Würtemberg damages, the veterinarian services of the Land asked the beekeepers to destroy feed combs because hive pollen was contaminated. The study of Chauzat et al, 2006[9], showed that Imidacloprid was detected in 40 pollen trap samples (81 samples were taken during this study, coming from 5 different regions). Imidacloprid persistence in the environment appears thus much more important than reported in the DAR (Draft Assessment Report).

11) The DAR does not include studies about the potential synergies between the active substance and bees pathogens. Imidacloprid shows such synergic properties with some pathogens agents[10]. In the case of bees this hypothesis has never been investigated in detail but is likely to occur with Nosema spp., and could explain the increase of bees pathologies noted by beekeepers and scientists during the last years. A PPP called Premise 200SC, whose active substance is Imidacloprid, is described as disorientating termites and making them ill by stopping the grooming behaviour. The PPP advertising paper explains that the grooming behaviour stopping allows soil fungi to attack termites. What about bees? Some hive micro-organisms are fungi, for instance the genius Nosema (usual pathogen of the bees) or Beauveria (in normal condition non-pathogen for bees). In the same paper we can read (last page) that "independent trials in Japan have Found Premise SC to be effective for at least five years". This fact is not in agreement the provided Imidacloprid DT50.

12) We have noticed amazing discrepancies between the results of the different tests: for example between the DL50 for honeybees and for wild bees (Bombus terrestris). Both studies (De Ruijter 1999, p. 913) conclude that Imidacloprid has effects for all tested doses, without correlation between the dose and the effect, including mortality. Similar discrepancies appear during cage, tunnel or field tests. Some tests highlight a lack of foraging activity (Bakker 2003, p. 943) where others find an increase of bee activity (Stadler 2000, p. 947). Such inconsistent results should be considered with caution: sufficient margins of security are necessary to consider the risk for bees. The conclusion on the acceptable risk for bees doesn't take such margins in account, since the figures accepted by the assessment report are a NOEC of 10 ppb, a nectar and pollen concentration of 5 ppb (the average of real concentration is 2 to 3.5 ppb, cfr. report of the French CST).

13) Importance of scientific studies validity criteria

a) The DAR considers the tests valid or not valid without having defined any validity criterion. The conclusions about the studies validity doesn't tally with those of the French Comité scientifique et technique, who has defined validity criteria. Invalidation of several studies as Guez et al. 2001, Suchail et al. 2001 or of results published by Pham-Delègue and Cluzeau 1999 is questionable when, for instance, the residues studies of Schmuck et al. (point B.9.4-5, p. 920) are considered valid, in spite of insufficient limits of detection (5 or 10 ppb). (Schmuck et al.) studies never detect any residue when other studies show a frequent presence of Imidacloprid in the foraged matrices (for instance, following a study about the pollen contaminations in France, Imidacloprid is detected in the half part of the trap pollen samples (40/81) 11). The methods used in this lab should be analysed in order to verify that they are able to detect actually the substances in the foraged matrices, particularly in the pollen since the potential contamination is inside the grains.

b) A statistic validation should be provided for the studies and their conclusions. Such validations are all the more necessary since the results variance is very great, for the acute and chronic LD50 and for the sub-lethal effects as well (see e.g. Kirchner 1998 and 2000, pp. 950 – 951).

14) We observe that the DAR dismisses all the studies that seem to be unfavourable to the molecule authorization, when the favourable studies obviously are not so carefully analysed from their validity point of view. Once time more this fact raises the problem of the scientific assessment independence since the assessment is integrally submitted by Ramakrishnan, R., Suiter, D.R, Nakatsu, C.H., Humber, R.A., and Bennett, G.W., 1999: Imidacloprid- Enhanced Reticulitermes flavipes (Isoptera: Rhinotermitidae) Susceptibility to the Entomopathogen Metarhizium anisopliae, J. Econ. Entomol. 92(5): 1125-1132 the applicant, without confirmation of any test by independent laboratories, even in case of doubt. In the current context, where seed coating insecticides remain the suspect number one in the worldwide bees mortalities, such a situation fosters suspicion, what is prejudicial to the beekeepers, to the concerned industry, and overall to the public authorities, which fail to ensure the general interest protection and the necessary arbitration between the interests of the concerned sectors.

The conclusion is very clear: the report evaluation doesn't respect Article 4 of Directive 91/414/CEE. It definitely fails to demonstrate that there is no unacceptable impact on bees or on other foraging species.

Moreover, the European Authorities have recently moved to offer greater support to the wider adoption of 'Integrated Pest Management' in the Framework Directive on the sustainable use of pesticides. The major advantage of integrated pest management is to avoid permanent pesticide residues in soils and plants that may lead to the development of resistant pest populations, as well as unwanted effects on human health. Using pesticides only when needed, against a well-defined pathogen, with limited effect on non-target species and during a limited period of time is the basement of integrated management. Seed coatings are just following the opposite approach: they are used in all case, even when there is no pathogen target to destroy. They use very persistent active substances in order to protect the plant from seeding to harvest. They remain in soil and plant for very long periods. They are not specific and destroy non-targets species.

Given the catalogue of serious flaws in the Commission's decision-making process PAN Europe wishes to request for a review of Regulation 149/208 and asks you to withdraw or suspend this Regulation in preventing harm to consumers.

Yours sincerely,
Stichting Natuur en Milieu,
Mirjam de Rijk
General Director

also on behalf of:
Ms. J. Kivits Inter Environment Wallonie, Belgium Mr. E. Cannell PAN-Europe, Pesticide Action Network Europe, England
M. F. Veillerette MDRGF, Mouvement pour le droit et le respect des générations futures, La France
M. F. Giot Nature et Progres, Belgium

References:
1   E.g. Bonmatin J-M, Marchand P., Charvet R, Moineau I,. Bengsch E.R.,Colin M-E. Quantification of imidacloprid uptake in maize crops.

2   Alix, A., and Vergnet, Chr., 2007: Risk assessment to honey bees: a scheme developed in France for non-sprayed systemic compounds, Pest Manag Sci.63: 1069 – 1080

3   For instance, refer to : Alix, A., and Vergnet, Chr., 2007: Risk assessment to honey bees: a scheme developed in France for non-sprayed systemic compounds, Pest Manag Sci.63: 1069-1080, point 4.2.

4   CST (non daté): Imidaclopride utilisé en enrobage de semences (Gaucho®) et troubles des abeilles – pp. 50 and 61.

5   Rortais A, Arnold G, Halm MP, Touffet-Briens F, 2005 : Modes of honeybees exposure to systemic insecticides : estimated amounts of contaminated pollen and nectar consumed by different categories of bees, Apidologie 36 (2205), 71 – 83

6   Alix, A., and Vergnet, Chr., 2007, op. cit. Halm, M.P., Rortais, A., Arnold, G., Taseï, J.N., Rault, S., 2006: New Risk Assessment Approach for Systemic Insecticides: The Case of Honey Bees and Imidacloprid (Gaucho), Environ. Sci. Technol. 2006, 40, 2448-2454

7   CST, 2004? (non daté): Imidaclopride utilisé en enrobage de semences (Gaucho®) et troubles des abeilles - Rapport final

8   Greatti, M, , Sabatini, A.G., Barbattini R., Rossi S., Stravisi A., 2003 : Risk of environmental contamination by the active ingredient imidacloprid used for corn seed dressing. Preliminary results, Bulletin of Insectology 56 (1): 69-72 Greatti M., Barbattini R., Stravisi A., Sabatini A.G., Rossi S., 2006 : Presence of the a.i. imidacloprid on vegetation near corn fields sown with Gaucho® dressed seeds, Bulletin of Insectology 59 (2): 99-103.

9   Chauzat, M.P., Faucon, J.P., Martel, A.C., Lachaize, J., Cougoule, N., Aubert, M., 2006: A survey of pesticides residues in pollen loads collected by honey bees in France, J. Econ. Entomol. 99 (2): 253 - 262

10 voir par exemple : Cuthbertson AG, Walters KF and Deppe C., 2005: Compatibility of the entomopathogenic fungus Lecanicillium muscarium and insecticides for eradication of sweet potato whitefly, Bemisia tabaci. Mycopathologia. 2005 Aug;160(1):35-41

11 Chauzat, M.P., Faucon, J.P., 2007: Pesticide residues in beeswax samples collected from honey bee colonies (Apis mellifera L.) in France, Pest Management Sci, 63: 1100–1106.

POTS SUPPLIED

John Kinross

Bee Books New and Old

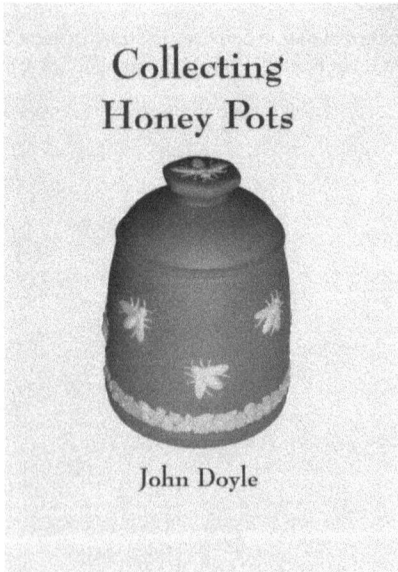

Collecting
Honey Pots

John Doyle

Many years ago we went to a B&B in South Cornwall for a holiday. My mother was concerned by the "Pots Supplied'" notice by the desk. Sure enough, as there was no indoor toilet, we were each given a pot to go under the bed. Hopefully, the Tourist Board, by now, has crossed this place off their list.

The time has come for members of the TARANOV Board to look at the current selection of new books. Ina Strainer has come up with "Collecting Honey Pots" (BB-NO, £5.40) as she is an avid collector has boxes of honey-pots, some still with honey in them - in her attic, but not under her bed. John Doyle, the author, is a schoolmaster who for relaxation edits the European Honey Pot Collecors Society magazlne. The book has 16 colour plates, one of which shows a "Lefton" pot from the USA. The Professor says that the owner found it on a train hence its name, but I never yet met an American who used the railway in USA, which is a pity as we enjoy railway travel here, even though it does cost more to park at the station than to ride on the train.

From Northern Bee Books come two interesting items. Paul Mann's "How to keep bees without finding the Queen" (NBB £6.00) reads well and is quite short. The illustratlons are useful and Paul comes from a family of beekeepers, whlch is really the best way to start. Perhaps an index and a bibllography would be useful if there is a reprint.

Of more meat is Dr Woodward's book "Queen Bee: Biology, Rearing & Breeding'" from New Zealand (NBB, £l5.00). It is very up-to-date and has colour pictures including some showing instrumental insemination equipment. The table of contents is helpful and the layout follows the same arrangement as the Beekeeping Study Notes (Yates & Yates) so that all paragraphs are numbered. Thls is a tlmely book as a lot of beekeepers are going in for queen rearlng, it seems.

From IBRA comes "Honey Farmer at Large" by Oliver Field (IBRA, £5.95) which is a series of chapters on his beekeeping experiences in unlikely places like Yemen, Mongolia, Egypt, Cameroon and Poland. The book is good value but from a design point-of-view it needs wider gutters as the perfect binding does not allow it to open enough to read very easily.

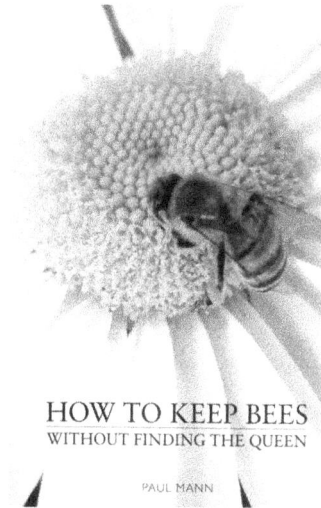

HOW TO KEEP BEES
WITHOUT FINDING THE QUEEN

PAUL MANN

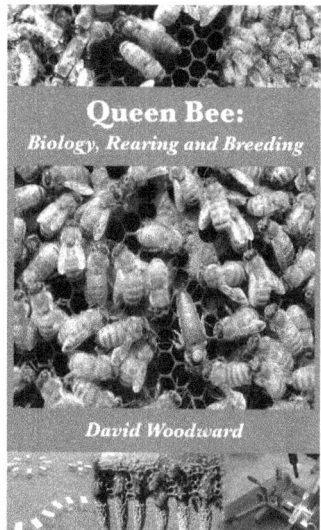

Queen Bee:
Biology, Rearing and Breeding

David Woodward

L.E. SNELGROVE | THE INTRODUCTION OF QUEEN BEES

L.E. SNELGROVE | QUEEN REARING

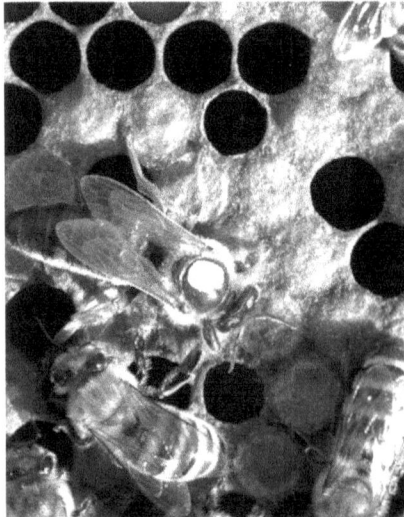

As regards reprints, NBB have done us a service by re-issuing Snelgrove's "Queen Rearing" and "The Introduction of Queen Bees" (both £15) which every beekeeper should have on the shelf, along with "Swarming" last reprinted by BBNO in 2007 for £9.95. It has a useful introduction by Karl Showler who says "it brings so much together in one place". Another reprint of much value, with a good index, is Steve Taber's "Breeding Super Bees" (NBB, £12.50) which, although American, has some useful suggestions for everyone else. Ina says she was taught to keep her back straight at school by carrying books on her head (see p.130, where Steve keeps his back straight while manipulating hives) and she dropped a large bIble on her teacher's foot which caused an uproar and meant sitting in the corner for one lesson.

BREEDING
SUPER BEES

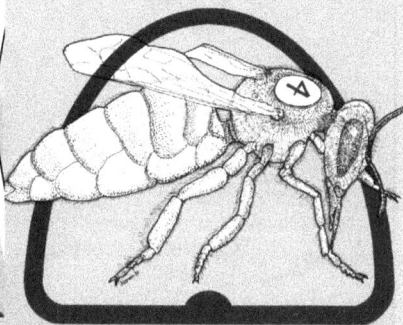

STEVE TABER

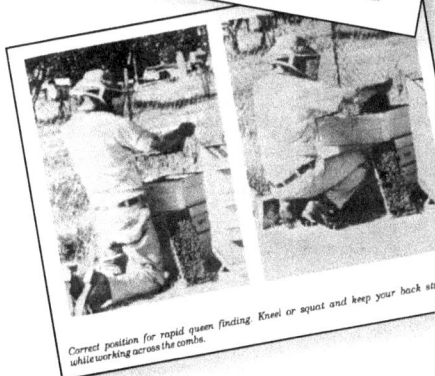

Correct position for rapid queen finding. Kneel or squat and keep your back str
while working across the combs.

A
COMPLETE GUIDE
for the
MANAGEMENT
of
BEES
Throughout the Year

by
DANIEL WILDMAN

Printed for the Author, and Sold by him, at his
Bee and Honey Warehouse, No 326, Holborn.
Where any Quantity of his New-invented Hives
may be had on the Shortest Notice
M.DCC.LXXX.
[Price One Shilling and Sixpence]

Rather unusual reprints have come from Lulu Publications. Firstly, Daniel Wildman"s "A complete guide for the management of bees'" (1770, originally costing one shilling and sixpence; now, in 2008, £6.95) which reads well today and I like the idea of using a very large spoon to rescue a swarm. We only have a large silver ladle and I'm not sure if I would be allowed to use it for a swarm.

The Beekeepers Alphabet

Price One Shilling

PURE HONEY EXTRACTED

John Whitby & Son
Printers & Publishers
Cornhill
Bridgwater

LONDON: SIMPKIN, MARSHALL & Co., 4, STATIONERS' HALL COURT

Of more amusement is "The Beekeeper's Alphabet" by Rev. Anderson, the first Hon. Secretary of Somerset Beekeepers (1886). For anyone who wants to know how Victorian beekeepers managed with "their racks, bell-jars, Ligurian bees etc, this is the book to get (BBNO, £.5.99), but the author didn't remaln Hon. Sec. for very long and soon the Somerset BKA had to be re-formed.

Finally the Professor has come up with a story his father heard whilst he was beekeeping in Africa. Two chiefs went to visit a fellow chief who was known to be a bit of a miser. He lived in a grass hut and was supposed to have a throne made of solid gold. When they reached his village there he was standing by the entrance of his hut. There was no sign of the throne whlch he had hldden away somewhere. They soon found out, however, for the wind got up, the hut swayed about and the throne came down trom above the door and flattened the miser chief. The moral of the story is, according to the Professor, that people in grass houses shouldn't stow thrones.

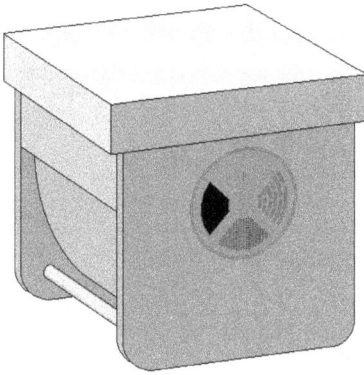

THE NEW AGE OF TOP BAR BEEKEEPING

Editor and David Cushman

In the 1960's there was a resurgence in the use of top bar hive hives, primarily as a simple method of keeping bees in countries where much beekeeping development was being carried out. Pioneers of this type of beekeeping included Penelope Papadopoulo, from Greece, who worked in Rhodesia (Zimbabwe), and Messrs Tredwell and Paterson, from Hampshire College of Agriculture, for use in Kenya. All three of these beekeepers carefully studied the early Greek beekeeping using basket hives with top bars and moveable combs as described in some detail by Sir George Wheeler (A Journey into Greece, published in 1682), which he saw in abundance at St Syriacus Monastery on Mount Hymettus, in Attica. By adopting the method of making hives with sides sloping inwards, homes for bees could be made from a variety of cheap materials found locally in the developing countries whilst giving the beekeepers full control of the bees and independent of the expense of modern beekeeping equipment. Since that time not only have beekeepers in many parts of the world benefited from this simple and cost effective method of beekeeping, but also there has been a trend for beekeepers in the developed world to use and modify top bar hives to fit in with their own management systems.

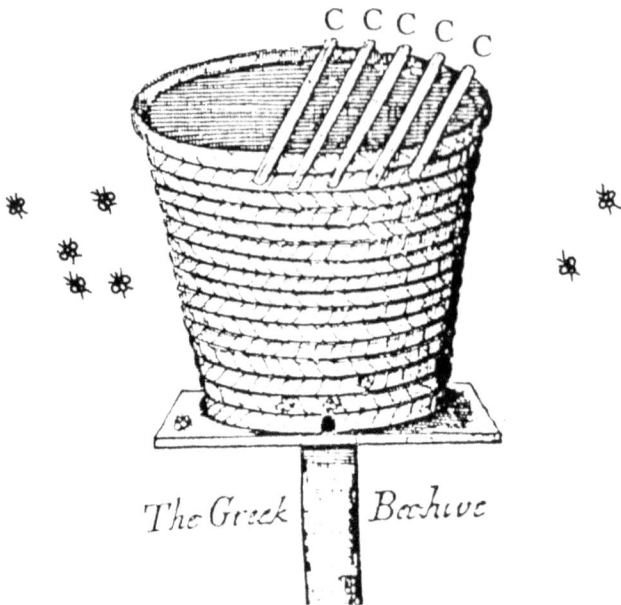

AN EARLY GREEK TOP BAR BASKET HIVE AS USED AT THE MONASTERY OF ST SYRIACUS.
(FROM A JOURNEY INTO GREECE, BY SIR GEORGE WHEELER).

In the early 1970's, I was fortunate to meet an elderly beekeeper who was more interested in trying out new ideas than just keeping his bees for honey production. Amongst some of the things he let me play with was one of Wood's early models of the Apidictor and later, to my surprise he gave me a colony of bees in a strange hive: Bill Beilby's Catenary Hive. In order to get it home, two of us had to manhandle it down a rather long ladder, for it was in a school apiary on top of the flat roof of the physics laboratory. At my first inspection I was surprised to see the enormous perfectly-shaped combs in the catenary-shaped brood chamber which gave 50% more space to the colony than the bees had in a National Hive. Bill Bielby, the CBI for Yorkshire, had designed the hive for its simplicity in structure and because it gave the bees the chance to build their combs in the way nature intended them to be, as well as making it a hive which beekeepers could use without having to buy frames and foundation. To give additional strength to the combs, pieces of nylon which had been immersed in hot wax were fastened to the top bars. In the hive which I was given, wire was fastened around. Whilst excluders and supers of National hive dimensions fitted on to the top of the Catenary hive, he also showed that honeycombs could be built and harvested from top bars only, the honey to be squeezed out from a suspended muslin bag using hinged wooden battens. Later on, I enjoyed making one of these hives, the plans of which - and his ideas for a simplified way of beekeeping - were published in his book 'Home Honey Production' in 1977. Whilst initially not truely a top-bar hive, it developed into one having utilised the principle of the early Greek hives and brought to the front a method of sustainable home beekeeping. The plans for Bielby's hive are from his book and additional material here on the Catenary hive is from David Cushman's excellent website, lineone.net/~dave.cushman/catenary.html

As I have no personal experience of this type of hive... the following text is transcribed mainly from Len Heath's book "A Case of Hives".

It was designed by Bill Bielby, in 1968, when he was County Beekeeping Lecturer for West Yorkshire. It was made for several years by a Yorkshire firm. It is quite unusual in shape and derives its name from the mathematical curve taken by a freely hanging rope or chain suspended from two points. The entrance is through a plastic disc mounted high up on one flat side, so that the eleven short-lugged frames are aligned the 'warm way' across the line of entry.

Originally the frames were accurately made to fit the curve of the box (with normal bee-space around) but later top bars alone were used, as it was realised that bees do not fasten combs to sloping side walls.

This unusual brood box had the same top rim size as a standard National box and a normal queen excluder and National (or British Commercial) super, would sit on top of it, but of course the unique shape of the brood combs makes such operations as Demaree(ing) or Snelgroving impossible.

The rationale behind the Catenary is that: - in nature bees will make comb of this shape in any cavity that is large enough, and it was observed that the bees built up well in spring. It was claimed that swarming was less, but Len Heath's experience, with two such hives over several years failed to support this.

Over several years other snags became evident. For example a large surface area of comb on the outer face of the first frame becomes propolised over and goes out of use if bees can fly straight in and on to it. A small modification involving a plywood baffle plate fixed internally opposite the entrance, a bee-space proud of the inner wall, effectively prevents this (and direct draught as well). More serious was the accumulation of debris and condensed water in the narrow base of the Catenary itself; this was corrected by cutting a half-inch (12 mm) drainage hole (loosely plugged with coarse wire wool) at the lowest point. Unfortunately both of Len's hives rotted at the base after about ten years and had to be scrapped. He claims to have enjoyed using them, as an interesting variant, and would have happily bought another if they were still available. He reports that they were easy to move to the heather and attracted much comment from other beekeepers, but that he could not recommend them for general use.

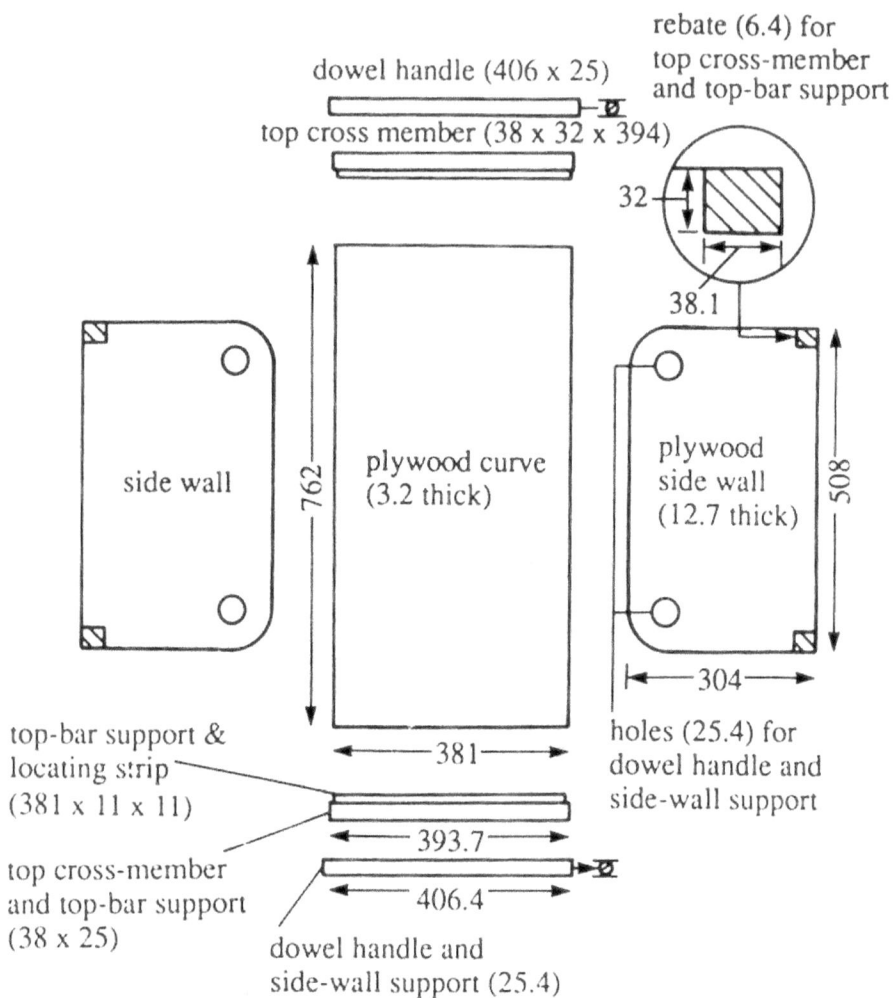

dowel handle (406 x 25)

rebate (6.4) for top cross-member and top-bar support

top cross member (38 x 32 x 394)

32

38.1

side wall

762

plywood curve (3.2 thick)

plywood side wall (12.7 thick)

508

304

top-bar support & locating strip (381 x 11 x 11)

top cross-member and top-bar support (38 x 25)

381

393.7

406.4

holes (25.4) for dowel handle and side-wall support

dowel handle and side-wall support (25.4)

COMPONENTS OF BIELBY'S CATENARY HIVE

THE SCOTTISH
Beekeeper

Magazine of
The Scottish
Beekeepers
Association

SEPTEMBER 2009

Published Monthly

Annual Membership £25 includes Magazine post paid U.K

SBA WEBSITE: http://www.scottishbeekeepers.org.uk

Registered Charity Number - SCO 0934

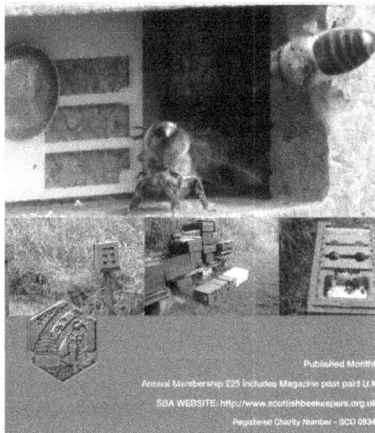

BEEKEEPING PRACTICES OLD, NEW AND 'GET AWAY WIE YE!'

ERIC McARTHUR

The Varroa mite has caused a fundamental rethink for many beekeepers of the pre Varroa generation, in Scotland anyway.

The new generation of beekeepers who have never had the pleasure of working with bees prior to Varroa just accept the mite as the norm and get on with the job.

In the halcyon days Swarm Prevention was the prime mover in good beekeeping husbandry, unlike our counterparts South of the Border, who had a much higher incidence of disease due to a higher stocking density of colonies with which to contend. The incidence of disease among Scotland's colonies was and still is relatively low compared to England.

However, Varroa changed all that!

During the early 70s and right up until April 1992, when the mite was discovered at Cockington in Devon, I was one of the few beekeepers in Scotland specifically breeding and selling queen bees and nucleus stocks throughout the UK. At that time British Rail had a Red Star service whereby a box of bees could be taken to the Central Station, Goods Inward department in Glasgow for next day delivery to virtually any rail station in the UK. The Post Office accepted Queen Bees in postal cages then and still does. A queen

31

mailed 1st Class would be with her new master within two days, correctly timed delivery to the Post Office counter could have the lady delivered by next post.

There was always an initial problem with the counter staff who seeing the legend "CARE - Queen Honey Bee" on the small package for that first time recoiled instinctively in horror. Thereafter, as a regular customer I had no further problems, in fact it became a highlight of the day for the counter staff when they had bees to deal with - new counter staff had to be 'broken in' each 'first time' or when a different Post Office was used!

Realising that beekeepers were the major problem in spreading the mite I ceased trading in bees immediately the Cockington event was promulgated in February 1992! At no small financial loss, I would add!

However, at that time the Anti Varroa Lobby of which I was President and Secretary was in full flood; so I bit the bullet, despite Scotland being well out of the SAI (Statutory Infested Area) designated along Southern English coastal counties at that time.

Even as beginner beekeeper in the late 60s I realised it was easier to produce queen bees than it was to get a honey crop and having this overwhelming need to possess as many bee colonies as possible and as quickly as possible I financed this need by rearing and selling queens and nuclei.

Despite having been in beekeeping, at a semi commercial level, for many years - now retired; the extreme pleasure, nay ecstasy, of, after making up a queenless nucleus and seeing eggs and young larvae in these nucs, on schedule, is as satisfying today as it ever was in those early years.

During those heady pre Varroa days I experimented with the limitations of queen rearing - how early to start and how late to stop - and also experimented with different methods of introducing queens into colonies in different states of queenrightness or queenlessness.

At one point in the mid 70s I even approached Mr Robertson, the proprietor of the then Steele and Brodie bee supply business at Newport on Tay, offering to supply Scottish bees in four frame nuclei as early as late April to supplement the trade in nuclei from France, which was the chosen exporting country for supplying the Scottish market; only to be told "Don't be daft, this can't be done". The fact was that I had already been supplying nucs to beekeepers in Scotland for a couple of years at this point. A check on the 1972 onward Spring advertisements in the Scottish Beekeeper will confirm this.

One extremely positive spin-off from early queen rearing was the facility to be able to requeen every strong hive by around the third week in May - before the bees had made any swarm preparations. Again I was informed that I was 'off my head'. However, the advantage of early requeening, which I practiced for many years in May in the 70s, when May, did what was expected of May was that once these strong colonies had a new queen, which of course is a veritable carboxylic acid, pheromone factory, by giving the colonies 'adequate room for expansion - viz at least 3 supers (first one drawn comb), the need to carry out the 7 day Swarm Inspection procedure became superfluous - these current year queens were a breakthrough which permitted me to expand to running around 80 colonies single handed while still working full time in shipbuilding.

I worked a system of requeening which I fondly called the Relay Requeening Method, which was severely criticised by Bernhard Mobus at the time (personal correspondence).

The accepted wisdom of those days was that some days should elapse after dequeening a colony before a new queen could be successfully introduced. Using a simple pulp matchbox I introduced the new queen immediately on removal of the original queen, which incidentally would still be only some 14 months old. These young queens were accepted and laying well within a few hours of introduction, and the matchbox 'cage' was deposited as pulp at the hive entrance by the following morning.

The acceptance rate of these new queens was almost 100%. The replaced queens were sold or given away as year old queens with a lot of mileage still in them and their quality was renowned North and South of the border.

A question I always asked of a beekeeper requesting a queen was "Are you certain that the colony is queenless?" I lost count of the number of times, after them being advised to insert a test comb of eggs and open brood into the colony, of the astonished result for the beekeeper, of this simple test - many of these colonies had virgins which had not started to lay on schedule - whether due to tardy mating due to unfavourable weather or beekeeper impatience. This simple test saved not only beekeeper cash but the life of a valuable queen. When in doubt - think ahead.

Having a sizeable number of colonies, without being overwhelmed with work, can be very reassuring.

My queen rearing in the 70s commenced mid March - again a loony idea as far as the accepted wisdom of the day was concerned - however, by observing colony development week by week from mid February onward the most prolific colonies can be easily identified. These colonies received a drawn drone comb right into the centre of the brood nest in mid March and each colony was fed copiously with 1:1 sugar syrup.

My opinion for what it is worth is that the bee colony will not start drone rearing, which is the first action in swarm preparation, until it is feeling prosperous - the observed vigour of the selected colonies demonstrated that given the more than adequate food supply they would do the business and that is just how it panned out.

I could have drones flying in late April most years - at one of the Autumn Conferences at Auchincruive in the 70s I mentioned to Bob Couston that I had been able to get a few queens mated and laying by 7th May that year - he gave me a look which needed no words. Ian Maxwell castigated me at the same Conference when at dinner on the Friday night he castigated me in front of the assembled diners by scorning me because I had said that I had successfully reared good quality queens using 4 frame nuclei. He said that the queens from emergency queen cells was, as far as he was concerned, doomed to be inferior. Such is the need to take the maverick down.

At that time I had not read Doolittle's work in America - this man made a fortune marketing queens reared under the emergency impulse - but Ian Stirrat, the Auchincruive apiarist of the day, later spoke to me about Doolittle's work and reckoned that Ian was not being honest - to say the least. I wonder if you still remember that one Ian!

Having had a deal of experience raising drones and queens, I again fell foul of a respected member of the beekeeping educational establishment, who, at a recent lecture to the Autumn Convention again at Auchincruive made a statement that the drone honeybee did not reach sexual maturity until it was 58 days old. I questioned this and it was not received well. Astonishingly, many beekeepers do not seem to realise the critical importance of the time taken for drone maturity. In fact the drone only lives around 55 days.

I used the 38 day drone sexual maturation period with good effect right from the start of my breeding phase.

After seeding the colonies in mid March with drone comb, I would check perhaps a week later for drone eggs laid - on seeing drone eggs I would count 17 days and commence queen rearing - by making up a 4 frame nucleus with one frame of sealed brood, one frame of eggs and open brood and two good store combs - all well covered in bees. This nuc was fed copiously! Four days later this nuc would be checked for queen cells! The bees did not always oblige and if that first cycle failed to produce queen cells by day 5 the failed comb was removed and replaced by a fresh comb until the bees told me they were ready to co-operate.Thereafter, a 4 frame nuc would be made up every two or three days. Once queen cell production has started, with the right beekeeper attitude and sufficient equipment, literally dozens of queens can be produced by making up sufficient numbers of 3 frame mating nuclei and harvesting, using a scalpel, the surplus queen cells from these 4 frame nucs, similar to a conveyor belt system.

Having a 4 frame nucleus for virtually every strong colony of bees imparts a marvellous sense of security - it did for me anyway - come hell or high water there was always a fall back to compensate for that poor performing queen, or the colony that suddenly and inexplicably goes queenless or perhaps the loss of a prime swarm before the late summer nectar flows start - a powerful 4 frame nuc introduced at the strategic moment will act like a blood transfusion and reinstate such a colony to honey gathering strength.

Incidentally, the counting of 17 days prior to beginning queen rearing makes it possible to have drone maturity coincide with queen sexual maturity, which occurs 21 days from egg laid in queen cell. For the arithmetically minded

17+21 = 38, the number of days for drone maturation. Sorry about that.

I spent part of my summer holidays with Athole Kirkwood, of Heather Hills Honey Farm at Bridge of Cally in 1972 and learned more in that short interlude than I could ever have from 10 years of reading books on managing bees. Athole managed some 2000 colonies at this time; working solely for honey - rasps and heather were his main honey sources; this was in the hey day of the soft fruit industry in Central Scotland. Legend had it that Athole could observe vegetation development in early spring in his area and predict almost to the hour when the rasps would bloom - he was indeed a superlative beekeeper - and one of the first to dare to take on the Scottish climate and make a living from honey production alone.

Athole used a particular swarm prevention technique which entailed caging the queen, at the first indication of swarming, in a special cage made from queen excluder. This cage was fixed to the underside of the top bar of a brood comb in the brood nest after which the colony was left for eight days then revisited and all queen cells cut down.

The queen remained caged for a further period of 14 days, then was released. Occasionally a queen would be rejected by the bees but the high rate of success of this method reduced the work load of swarm control and swarm prevention and suited Athole's management needs.

Despite the cage procedure being successful I felt that the method was not the one for me. If a quick calculation is done the beekeeper will discover that during the three week confinement period - at a laying rate of 1500 eggs per day - the loss of potential bee numbers amounts to some 31,500 bees! I modified Athole's system by, instead of confining the queen in a cage I confined her in a queen holding nuc, a 'queen reservoir'. This nuc consisted of the swarm queen on a frame of sealed brood with sufficient bees to well cover the brood and one more 'frame of stores covered in bees, for good measure. An empty frame on either side of the two occupied frames completed the 4 frame nuc, which is an ideal size for transporting and not too 'greedy' for bees. This nuc was taken away to an out apiary and fed; and within a month was bursting with bees and as a tool could be used for all kinds of different procedures - especially if the queen was born in the latter part of the previous year, that is a queen in her second season but still only one year old or younger.

There are so many different and exciting procedures which can be used to bend the honey bee to our will - the beekeeper only has to remember that the bee like ourselves is 'only the equivalent of being human' and cannot be forced to perform tasks out-with her natural limitations - it is up to the progressive, inquisitive and dare I say it, intelligent beekeeper to explore these limits and become a better beekeeper in the process. To such adventurous folk I say; "Follow your instincts and observe the feed back from the bees and forget the limited 'accepted wisdom' of so many who would be your advisors."

One of these accepted wisdoms from a past era is that over-wintering a colony headed by a queen bee entering her second winter is acceptable good practice.

Karl Pfefferle, a much respected German Commercial Beekeeper, after many years experience of 'living' with Varroa, advocates that the best defence against the mite is correct anti Varroa treatment backed up by over-wintering colonies headed by a vigorous, current year queen - as opposed to a one year old+ queen, about to enter her second winter and which has probably been severely stressed by mite parasitisation during her short life.

How many beekeepers reading this have already witnessed queens carrying at least one mite on their bodies? I have spoken to beekeepers who talk of noting several mites riding on the queen. These little fiends are not playing Cowboys and Indians; they are sucking the vitality out of your best hope of getting your bees through the winter - alive.

Think about it and start rearing your own quality replacement queens - it is so simple.

Reprinted from The Scottish Beekeeper, September 2009,
with kind permission of the author and editor.

6. A 'field' bee delivers her load to either a house bee or direct into a cell.

THE HONEY FACTORY (HOW BEES TURN NECTAR INTO HONEY)

BILL CLARK, CAMBRIDGE BKA

●

Back in the spring of 1995 at our monthly Cambridgeshire BKA Committee meeting, we were casting our minds around for a suitable display/theme for that year's Honey Show - one of the attractions at the August Bank Holiday, 'Fenland Country Fair'. Staging and judging was on the Saturday and open to CBKA members late afternoon/early evening, then on the Sunday and Monday of the Fair, it was open to the paying public. As one of the practical members, who usually got down to producing this section of the show, much was expected from me; however on this occasion little was forthcoming. At past shows, we had gone through the whole gamut of showing folk the different aspects of beekeeping with, as always, one, two, and even three observation hives in attendance. Bob Lemon, our Chairman at the time, suggested that as we had previously shown the importance of bees in pollination, perhaps we should also explain how the bees made honey, finally remarking, "When folk realise what a natural product it is, it can only be good for honey sales." I am afraid I didn't like the idea at all! "Mr Chairman, about 90% of the visitors to our show know zilch about the countryside; can you please spare a moment to listen to me harking back to 1941? We had two boy evacuees from London billeted on us, and on their first morning, I, a younger eight year old, took them

37

to see the pigs. First, all they could say was, 'Err,r what a stink!' And second, 'Why do you keep them?' They were horrified when I told them that their bacon at breakfast had come from some earlier pigs, and said they would never eat bacon again! But worse was to come. When I took them with me to collect the hens' eggs, one was still sitting in a nesting-box, and as I moved her to take the eggs, one wet egg, with a spot of blood on it, slid out of her bottom. I can guess what those lads wrote to their parents because only weeks later they returned home, obviously thinking war-torn London was safer than our ghastly countryside. If we describe in detail how bees suck up nectar, and regurgitate it from bee to bee and cell to cell to make honey, our sales will plummet!" With that, our dear Chairman commented, "Can we all put some thought to our display between now and the next meeting please," and moved on to the next item on the agenda.

Besides looking after our lovely countryside, a large part of my work involved explaining it to school groups - and from time to time making a set piece that they could learn from whilst eating their lunch or sheltering from a shower. Despite being aimed at the children, parents and teachers were often heard discussing some aspect that they hadn't known about. Could something similar be done with honey making? I phoned Bob, and apologised for shooting down his suggestion, adding that I would apply all my spare time to the task, and by 'hook or by crook', have it ready for the show. I wanted it to be mainly visual and child attention grabbing, with concise explanation to involve the adults - not bore them to tears. Finally the sequence of events was printed out; now for the graphics - should it be photos, or could I lift my drawing skills a notch or two? Then one evening, as I tossed yet another rather ugly looking 'cartoon' bee in the bin, my eyes passed over the furry bee/paper clip clutching a stick of rock - bought from our CBKA honey stall during that afternoon, and awaiting my granddaughter's next visit. My mind went into overdrive! I rushed to the phone, "John, those sticks of rock with a bee attached, can I have a box at cost? Are there any larger bees? I need at least one." The good news was, he also had some bees that had lost their grip - a bit like yours truly - and gave me those, too, along with four or five small ones. With the bees chosen, it was simple to decide the cell size - with some poetic license for the frame size, so allowing room for all the paraphernalia as the ideas began to flow. The absolute truth was going to be told - how the bees make honey - but in a humorous, 'Honey Factory'.

Over the next weeks I trawled through my boxes of spares - others call them boxes of rubbish - and kept a more vigilant observation on our roadside lay-bys. They did indeed come up trumps, providing all the metal, plywood and hardboard needed: even a dumped radio, electric fire and a cooker supplied parts to make up the wind fan, suction tubes and heads for the vacuums, and the scouts hats - with a one metre scrap of 10 mm ribbed plastic conduit making the most lifelike grubs, when cut and bent to shape. There were a few problems making the cells, because of the need for the display to be easily transportable and light. Plywood cells 50 mm deep would add quite a bit to the weight, and so I finally opted for corrugated cardboard - smoothing "bath sealant" around the seams and edges to give a reasonable wax-like finish. Realising that I need only make cells that were to be 'open', saved further time and weight, and therefore I made a 50 mm deep cardboard box frame, and mounted it base outwards onto the hardboard backing. I then marked out the cells, decided which would be open - the brood would be a patch in the centre and a few open along the base - and cut out the shape of those only, the made-up cells were then fitted in the spaces. To make the cell shapes on the uncut portion of the frames, hexagons were cut out from a roll of thick kitchen paper which had a textured surface, very similar looking to brood cell surface. Using wallpaper paste, I layered one to three thicknesses over the rest of the cell-marked area - the wooden frame surround was painted in last! To make the paper shapes, I cut out two hexagonal pieces of hardboard of the appropriate size, folded the paper twenty times, clamped it between the two hexagons, cut round with a craft knife, and had twenty pieces ready for gluing. One difficulty was mixing paint that dried wax and honey coloured but at least the extra coats helped give texture.

It was great fun designing and building the air fan and the two different sized wooden derricks - all the wood for the derricks and swinging cradles will be recognised by older beekeepers, as parts from old fashioned frames. However, there are such a variety of small plastic toy cranes and such now, that there is no need to make one's own. The cylinder vacuum cleaners were made from doweling, plastic insulated wire, and the insulation off 'push on' electrical connectors, forming the cleaner body, vacuum tube, and suction head, in that order - for the use of the forager bees. Scouts and distributing bees use wooden spoons carved from doweling split down the centre. Pipes at the cell face were made from the type of plastic drinking straws with a bendy section, one extra long one is a couple joined, with the bendy sections either end - don't ask how the honey runs uphill! Only three bees were changed from the basic design: the large queen, who has a crown cut out of a plastic drink bottle top sprayed gold, a scout bee wearing a 'scout' hat, and another wearing both a scout hat and a 'Tou-tou', also on two upright legs - cut from a small plastic figure.

Sequence of numbered labels is as follows:

"NO 1. A 'SCOUT' BEE RETURNS TO THE HIVE WITH A SAMPLE OF NECTAR, AND/OR POLLEN." - held in a wooden spoon.

"NO 2. A 'FORAGER' HAS NOTED A SCOUT'S DANCE, AND FLIES STRAIGHT TO THE FLOWERS." - carrying a vacuum.

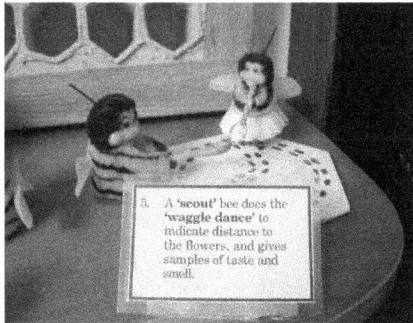

"NO 3. A 'FORAGER' WHILST RETURNING WITH NECTAR IS ALREADY MIXING ENZYMES INTO HER LOAD." - also carrying a vacuum. These three labels with the appropriate bees, are attached to a tight line that is fixed close by the waggle dancer, and angles across to the centre of a flower on the ceiling with the three bees suitably arranged, flying inwards or outwards. In the show marquee I used the services of a younger man to shin up the pole and clamp a large plywood flower at the top.

"NO 4, A YOUNG 'HOUSE' BEE PRACTICES LEAVING AND RETURNING TO THE HIVE BEFORE GOING OUT ON FIELD DUTIES." - is the only other bee outside the hive, and with her label, is attached to a 60 cm diameter spiral wire from the roof of the hive to the top of a thin cane. Her and the two scouts are

also the only three small sized bees used - I thought it was a shame not to make use of them!

"NO 5. A 'SCOUT BEE' DOES THE WAGGLE DANCE TO INDICATE DISTANCE TO THE FLOWERS AND GIVES SAMPLES OF TASTE AND SMELL." - this is placed on a small triangular upstand in front of the scout dressed in a 'Tou-tou', who for ease and clarity is fixed to the right hand side of the floor, rather than the face of the comb.

"NO 6. A 'FORAGER' DELIVERS HER LOAD TO EITHER A 'HOUSE' BEE, OR DIRECT INTO A CELL." - this is fixed to the floor on the left of the dancing bee, and is represented by a field bee carrying a vacuum, facing a house bee holding out a wooden spoon.

"NO 7. THE CELLS CHOSEN TO PLACE THE NECTAR ARE IN THE HOTTEST PART OF THE HIVE, WHICH IS IN AND AROUND THE BROOD NEST." - this is attached to the face of the brood comb, just to the right of a bee hanging in a cradle, and holding the mid-floor mounted derrick's bucket, against a cell. Central, above this area, a thermometer dial is set in the comb, showing 95f/32c.

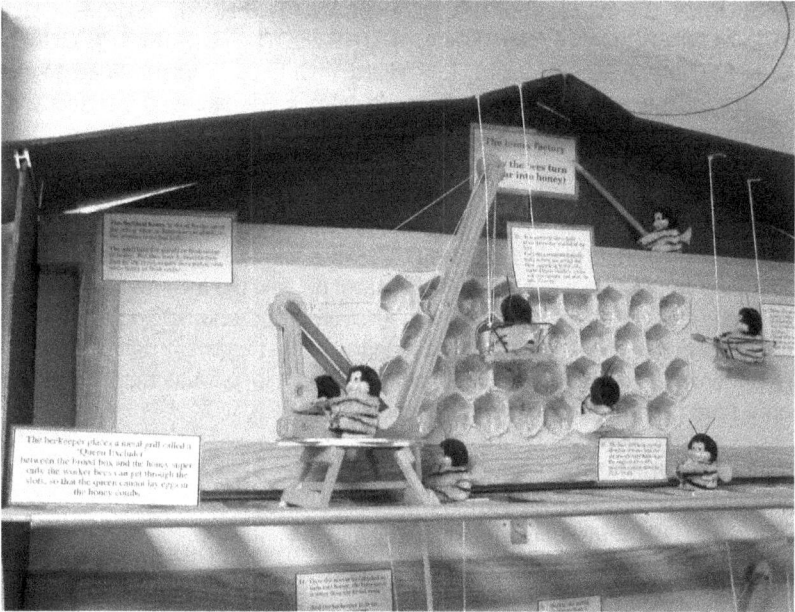

"NO 8. 'HOUSE' BEES THEN MOVE THE DROPLETS BETWEEN ONE ANOTHER, CELL TO CELL, AND IN AND OUT OF THEIR OWN HONEY CROPS, SO EXPOSING THE NECTAR TO THE DRYING AIR STREAM. (A HALF HOUR OF THIS TREATMENT REMOVES 5% OF THE MOISTURE, AND PUTS IN MOST OF THE ENZYMES." - this label is attached to the left hand side of the brood comb, just behind the fanning bees, and grouped around it are two bees on the floor, facing one another and holding wooden spoons, a bee on a cradle holding a tube from one cell to another and bees with bottoms sticking out of cells.

"NO 9. DURING THIS INITIAL TREATMENT HEAT IS NEEDED, ESPECIALLY TO CONVERT SUCROSE RAPIDLY INTO FRUCTOSE AND GLUCOSE." - this label is attached in the space to the left of the thermometer.

"NO 10. DURING A HEAVY NECTAR 'FLOW', SERRIED RANKS OF BEES KEEP FANNING, DAY AND NIGHT, TO REMOVE THE MOISTURE LADEN AIR. SOME FACING 'IN' ON ONE SIDE WHILST OTHERS FACE 'OUT' ON THE OTHER." - this label is fixed in front of four bees manning the fan; two facing in and two facing out, of course!

"No 11. THE BEEKEEPER PLACES A METAL GRILL CALLED A 'QUEEN

EXCLUDER' BETWEEN THE BROOD BOX AND THE HONEY SUPER; ONLY THE WORKERS CAN PASS THROUGH THE SLOTS, SO THAT THE QUEEN CANNOT LAY EGGS AMONG THE HONEY CELLS." - this is fixed to the surface of the excluder, which is made from hardboard and painted with aluminium paint.

"No 12. ONCE THE NECTAR HAS STARTED TO TURN INTO HONEY, THE BEES MOVE IT AWAY FROM THE BROOD AREA, AND THE BEEKEEPER PUTS ON ANOTHER HONEY SUPER." - this is fixed to the super comb face. Standing on the queen excluder is the smaller derrick, like the one below, being operated by two bees, one turning the windlass and one holding the tipping rope, again with a bee in a cradle holding the bucket against a cell. Below the excluder is one bee in a swinging cradle, holding a long tube from a cell in the brood comb up to one in the super comb.

"No 13. THE BEES KEEP MOVING DROPLETS OF HONEY INTO THE AIR STREAM - THEY HAVE TO GET THE ORIGINAL MOISTURE CONTENT OF 40 TO 80%, TO AROUND 17.5 TO 18.5%" - with the relevant bees moving honey around the comb.

"NO 14. IT IS NOW OVER THREE DAYS SINCE THE NECTAR ARRIVED AT THE HIVE. THE HONEY IS RIPENING NICELY, AND THE BEES ARE GIVING THE FINAL TOPPING UP OF THE CELLS. EACH OF THESE SHALLOW COMBS WILL NOW CONTAIN JUST OVER ONE KILO OF HONEY." - clear bath sealant was used to fill cells and spoons with nectar, whilst for those filled with honey, the sealant was painted honey colour.

"No 15. THESE CELLS NOW CONTAIN RIPE HONEY; IT WILL KEEP INDEFINITELY, PROVIDED THEY ARE CAPPED WITH WAX TO EXCLUDE THE AIR AND MOISTURE. (BROOD CELLS ARE CAPPED WITH A POROUS WAX/POLLEN MIX, TO ALLOW AIR INTO THE PUPAE)." - placed on the right-hand side of the patch of open cells; below it sits a bee in a hanging cradle, smoothing on the wax capping with a trowel.

"NO 16. THE FINISHED HONEY - USUALLY MUCH MORE THAN THE COLONY'S NEEDS - IS STORED FOR THEIR USE WHEN NO FLOWERS ARE AVAILABLE, OR THE WEATHER IS TOO INCLEMENT FOR FLYING. THE ADULT BEES LIVE MOSTLY ON FRESH NECTAR AT OTHER TIMES - THE NURSE BEES HAVE TO MANUFACTURE 'BROOD FOOD' FOR THE GRUBS, USING HIGH PROTEIN POLLEN AND ONLY A LITTLE NECTAR OR HONEY." - placed on the capped left-hand area - an afterthought, after I was approached whilst manning my observation hive at an 'Apple Day' by two 'Vegan ladies', who berated all beekeepers for stealing honey from the bees' babies!

The labels are neatly squared and given a black border - the numerals are essential to lead the reader along - the only un-numbered label is, "THE HONEY FACTORY. (HOW BEES TURN NECTAR INTO HONEY)" in the peak of the "pent" roof. Just to make sure you do not miss it, a bee sits just below pointing to it with a shiny red pencil!

As you can imagine, the display was only finished and ready for inspection after burning much midnight oil - and the day before our last Committee meeting prior to the Show. Conveniently, at that time we held our Committee meetings in the School Room at Wandlebury, only a short walk from my workshop, and it was placed against the wall in the L shaped room which would be its permanent home after the Show. As host, I was also engaged in readying the tea and biscuits in the little adjoining kitchen, but kept a weather eye on the arriving members! Not a word was said - other than, "good evening" and such, and not one set of footsteps did I hear stop by the display; in fact when I took my seat at the long table, all eyes seemed to be carefully aligned in any opposite direction, and I thought, "Oh dear, they hate it!" The meeting started in the usual way, and moved along from item to item until we got to the main business of the evening - the final preparations for the Show. "Well", exclaimed the Chairman, "You have all had chance to see Bill Clark's efforts, what do you think?" At that - a standing ovation, followed by a rush for a closer look! Not one dissenting voice, although I did hear comments such as: "I didn't know they did that?" or "So that's why there is often nectar among the brood?" It was even teaching the beekeepers!

It has made two or three trips to shows over the years, even another county BKA borrowed it for theirs. However, I was rather disappointed when I visited, for they had dispensed with the bee circling above the hive and the flower and the line to the roof - placing the returning scout, forager bees and labels on the floor of the hive, thus, making it look overcrowded and removing two of the highlights for the children. "Oh look Mummy, the bees are flying up to the flower." and, "There is one learning to fly!" A "Please do not touch", label is unfortunately very necessary, or little hands will completely rearrange the display in minutes - I discovered that the bath sealant was better to anchor down the bees, labels, and items that need it, also to fix the spoons, vacuums, ropes, and such to the bees "hands", for it gives a little more elasticity than a straight glue, but even so a glance is needed from time to time to put something back to rights. The photos of me working on the bees are a result of a recent need for replacement wings - chocolate box packing - and antennae - black plastic ties - and a good dusting and repaint. It is now a permanent wall fixture in the new, 'Education Centre' at Wandlebury, where each year, hundreds of school children - and teachers and parents - look, smile, and wonder at the marvel of honey bees.

I dare say, with all the computer power we now have at our disposal, it would be easy to go for a pictorial display; you could certainly download some good images, and probably make up some equally comical - and almost lifelike pictures of bees - working with real industrial equipment. However, I am finding it enough just to print the story, and am stopping right here and now!

BILL CLARK IN HIS WORKSHOP

BEEKEEPING: KEEP IT SIMPLE

THE TIMES BEE-MASTER FAVOURED SIMPLE
SKEP BEEKEEPING, IT WAS TO BE CONSIDERED
A VALUABLE ENTERPRISE FOR COTTAGERS NOT
A HOBBY FOR THE RICH WHO DABBLED AROUND
WITH FANCY HIVES OR USED BEES AS A MATTER OF
ENTOMOLOGICAL CURIOSITY.

'The object of my letters has been to open up to the cottager a means of revenue very agreeable, but very much neglected or mismanaged. I have directed your attention to bee-keeping not as a fancy pursuit, or as an interesting entomological investigation, but as a practical and real work.

Hence I have not discussed a variety of toys used as beehives, very pretty and tasteful to the eye of a sentimental apiarian, but so bothering to the bees that they wish such houses were at the bottom of the sea. Simplicity of structure, directness of use, and availableness for deprivation of honey and yet preservation of the honeymakers ought to be the guiding law. Bees don't like to be paid too many, too obsequious, or too patronizing attentions'.

Letters to the Editor
The Bee-Master's Sermon
From The Times, August 5th 1864

The Times Bee Master was John Cumming, a minister of the Scottish National Church, who contributed to the Field and Standard, as well as The Times. He preferred skep beekeeping, the honey being humanely harvested

**THE INTERIOR OF ALFRED NEIGHBOUR'S BEEHOUSE, FROM 'THE APIARY; OR, BEES, BEE-HIVES AND BEE CULTURE'
1865 - A PRIME EXAMPLE OF CUMMING'S SCORN AGAINST THE GROWING FASHIONS IN BEEKEEPING.**

by driving bees from the full hives. His correspondence was often of a heated nature being mostly directed at William Bernhard Tegetmeier, the founder of the Royal Entomological Society, a regular contributor to many newspapers and journals (until he was 90) and whose ideas disturbed Cummings immensely. Both of these opponents wrote books, Cumming: 'Beekeeping' by 'The Times' Bee-master, London, 1864 - which reflects some of the controversy, and Tegetmeier: 'Bees, hives and honey', London 1860.

WORDSEARCH

WITHIN THIS GRID ARE THE NAMES OF 49 AUTHORS OF BEE BOOKS FOR YOU TO FIND, SOME OLD SOME MODERN. GOOD LUCK.

```
M  E  T  C  A  L  F  E  I  P  E  T  T  I  G  R  E  W  E  H
G  O  V  B  P  L  S  L  A  K  C  N  I  L  R  E  T  E  A  M
A  L  E  S  S  A  R  G  D  O  N  S  O  X  N  W  Q  C  D  L
L  D  D  Q  V  S  I  M  M  I  N  S  N  E  R  I  T  E  B  I
T  T  A  D  K  P  R  Z  O  B  K  O  I  E  E  L  T  D  U  N
O  E  D  F  N  M  S  T  T  U  N  G  L  N  S  D  O  D  T  D
N  U  X  N  O  E  Y  D  W  R  H  L  M  A  A  M  B  E  L  A
H  T  H  X  T  H  E  G  E  B  I  A  P  R  R  A  B  G  E  U
O  B  C  U  S  D  K  V  O  P  D  L  A  C  F  N  A  D  R  E
O  T  S  T  U  O  K  U  S  A  V  L  G  S  L  A  D  E  N  R
P  H  I  W  O  R  R  I  B  B  A  N  D  S  C  E  B  W  H  P
E  O  R  I  C  R  H  S  I  U  H  P  E  P  H  Y  L  E  R  O
R  R  F  R  K  E  A  O  F  Y  X  Z  N  I  K  T  S  A  C  S
W  L  E  R  I  H  S  E  H  C  P  Y  E  L  I  A  B  B  E  W
E  E  I  Y  E  D  A  W  H  G  Y  D  Z  I  E  R  Z  O  N  T
D  Y  E  H  C  M  R  E  T  R  O  P  N  O  T  T  A  R  T  S
M  U  Q  P  N  K  Y  R  U  B  D  O  O  W  K  F  L  O  F  I
O  V  N  M  U  T  T  O  L  F  F  E  V  O  R  G  L  E  N  S
R  Y  E  L  N  A  M  N  K  E  V  A  N  S  T  L  O  G  A  N
E  U  R  J  E  K  F  R  E  E  S  E  G  G  I  D  W  C  O  Z
```

All you need to keep Bees well!

NATIONAL BEE SUPPLIES

Makers of the finest quality beehives

Everything for the new and experienced Beekeeper

Call us for expert advice and friendly service

10
DIARY & CALENDAR

- PART II -

*SR (SUNRISE) SS (SUNSET) FOR LONDON UK.

Notes and photographs by the Editor.

JANUARY

The careful insect 'midst his works I view, Now from the flowers exhaust
the fragrant dew, With golden treasures load his little thighs,
And steer his distant journey through the skies.

John Gay, Rural Sports (canto I, l. 82).

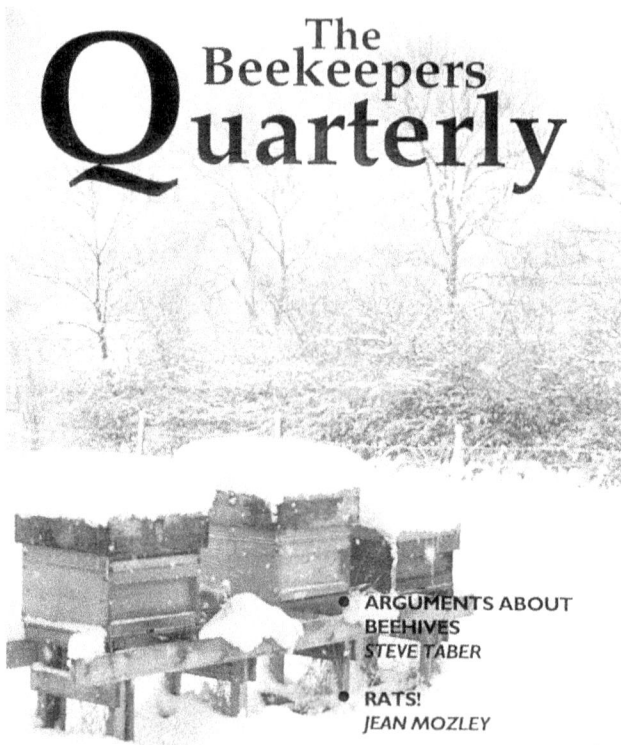

The Beekeepers Quarterly

- **ARGUMENTS ABOUT BEEHIVES**
  STEVE TABER

- **RATS!**
  JEAN MOZLEY

- **THE HOUSE THAT PETER BUILT**
  PETER KINSEY

- **LOOK LISTEN & LEARN**
  RON BROWN

Disturb the bees as little as possible. Some beekeepers put boards in front of the hive on sunny days when there is snow, so that the bees are not drawn out by the strong light only to be chilled and die when they fall in the snow.

DAY	JANUARY 2010 FORAGE	TEMP		WIND		CL'D	RAIN	1	2	3
		MIN	MAX	DIR	B.S			HIVE WEIGHT		
1										
2										
3										
4										
5										
6										
7										
8										
9										
10										
11										
12										
13										
14										
15										
16										
17										
18										
19										
20										
21										
22										
23										
24										
25										
26										
27										
28										
29										
30										
31										

JAN10

	8,FR
1,FR NEW YEAR'S DAY	9,SA SR 8.03, SS 4.10
2,SA SR 8.05, SS 4.02	10,SU
3,SU	**11,MO**
4,MO	**12,TU**
5,TU	**13,WE**
6,WE	**14,TH**
7,TH	**15,FR** ○

16,SA SR 7.58, SS 4.20	24,SU
17,SU	25,MO
18,MO	26,TU
19,TU	27,WE
20,WE	28,TH ◍
21,TH	29,FR
22,FR	30,SA SR 7.42, SS 4.44
23,SA SR 7.51, SS 4.32	31,SU

FEBRUARY

Bees work for man, and yet they never bruise
Their Master's flower, but leave it having done,
As fair as ever and as fit to use;
So both the flower doth stay and honey run.

George Herbert, The Church--Providence.

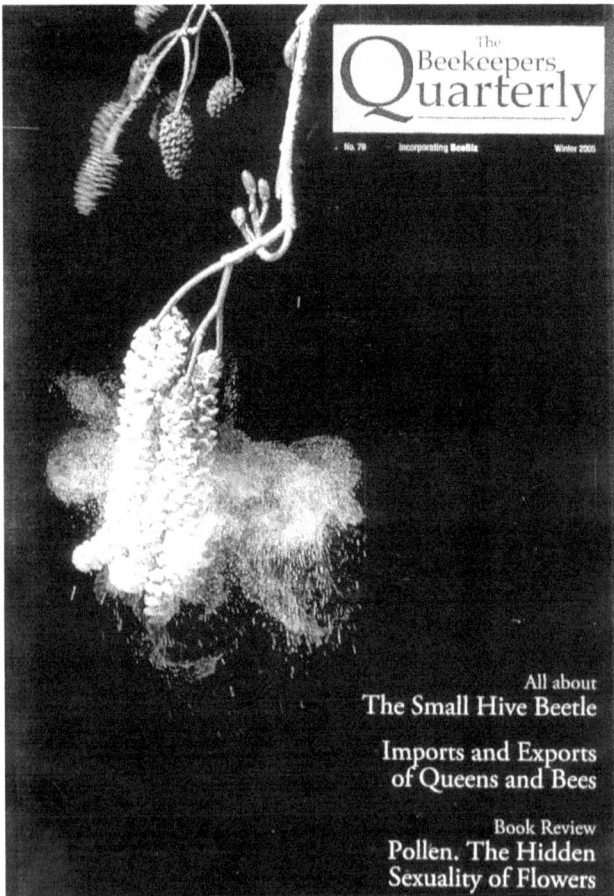

Many early sources of pollen are available to bees on mild days. Take notice which hives are taking in the most pollen - be suspicious of those with few or no pollen gatherers; these hives may be queenless. Heft hives to check if they need feeding.

DAY	FEBRUARY 2010 FORAGE	TEMP		WIND		CL'D	RAIN	1	2	3
		MIN	MAX	DIR	B.S			HIVE WEIGHT		
1										
2										
3										
4										
5										
6										
7										
8										
9										
10										
11										
12										
13										
14										
15										
16										
17										
18										
19										
20										
21										
22										
23										
24										
25										
26										
27										
28										

FEB10

	8,MO
1,MO	**9,TU**
2,TU	**10,WE**
3,WE	**11,TH**
4,TH	**12,FR**
5,FR	13,SA SR 7.18, SS 5.09
6,SA SR 7.30, SS 4.57	14,SU ○
7,SU	**15,MO**

16,TU	**24,WE**
17,WE	**25,TH**
18,TH	**26,FR**
19,FR	27,SA SR 6.50, SS 5.35
20,SA SR 7.04, SS 5.22	28,SU ◉
21,SU	
22,MO	
23,TU	

MARCH

Even bees, the little alms-men of spring flowers,
Know there is richest juice in poison-flowers.

Isaac Watts

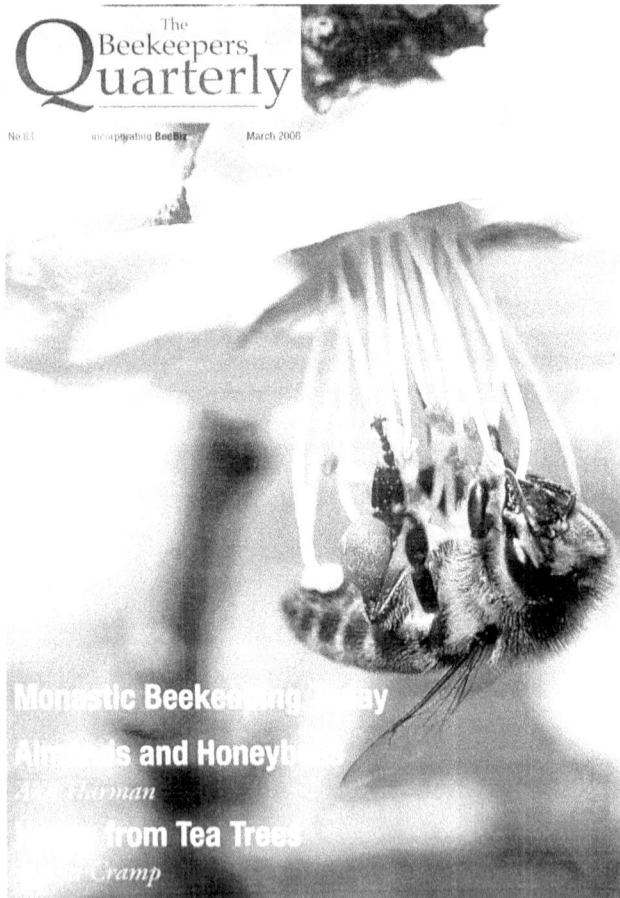

As the days lengthen and become milder, more forage sources become available for bees. However, brood rearing can soon deplete stores and many colonies can die of starvation at this critical time.

DAY	MARCH 2010 FORAGE	TEMP		WIND		CL'D	RAIN	1	2	3
		MIN	MAX	DIR	B.S			HIVE WEIGHT		
1										
2										
3										
4										
5										
6										
7										
8										
9										
10										
11										
12										
13										
14										
15										
16										
17										
18										
19										
20										
21										
22										
23										
24										
25										
26										
27										
28										
29										
30										
31										

MAR10

	8,MO
1,MO	**9,TU**
2,TU	**10,WE**
3,WE	**11,TH**
4,TH	**12,FR**
5,FR	13,SA SR 6.19, SS 5.59
6,SA SR 6.35, SS 5.47	14,SU
7,SU	**15,MO** ○

16,TU	**24,WE**
17,WE	**25,TH**
18,TH	**26,FR**
19,FR	27,SA ● SR 5.47, SS 6.23
20,SA SR 6.03, SS 6.11	28,SU
21,SU	**29,MO**
22,MO	**30,TU** ●
23,TU	**31,WE**

APRIL

The little bee returns with evening's gloom,
To join her comrades in the braided hive,
Where, housed beside their mighty honey-comb,
They dream their polity shall long survive.

Charles Tennyson Turner, A Summer Night in the Bee Hive.

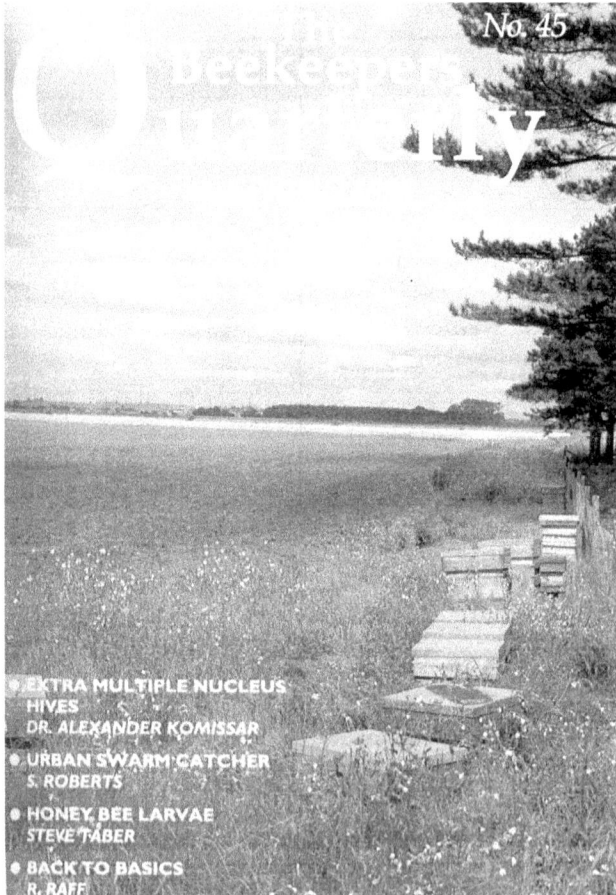

No. 45

EXTRA MULTIPLE NUCLEUS
HIVES
DR. ALEXANDER KOMISSAR

URBAN SWARM CATCHER
S. ROBERTS

HONEY BEE LARVAE
STEVE TABER

BACK TO BASICS
R. RAFF

The first fields of oil seed rape are beginning to show - ensure that supers are in place in readiness for an early crop of honey.

DAY	APRIL 2010 FORAGE	TEMP		WIND		CL'D	RAIN	1	2	3
		MIN	MAX	DIR	B.S			HIVE WEIGHT		
1										
2										
3										
4										
5										
6										
7										
8										
9										
10										
11										
12										
13										
14										
15										
16										
17										
18										
19										
20										
21										
22										
23										
24										
25										
26										
27										
28										
29										
30										

APR10

	8,TH
1,TH	**9,FR**
2,FR GOOD FRIDAY	10,SA SR 6.16, SS 7.46
3,SA SR 6.31, SS 7.35	11,SU
4,SU EASTER SUNDAY*	**12,MO**
5,MO	**13,TU**
6,TU	**14,WE** ○
7,WE	**15,TH**

16,FR	24,SA SR 5.46, SS 8.10
17,SA SR 6.00, SS 7.58	25,SU
18,SU	**26,MO**
19,MO	**27,TU**
20,TU	**28,WE** ◉
21,WE	**29,TH**
22,TH	**30,FR**
23,FR	* ORTHODOX EASTER

MAY

In the nice bee, what sense so subtly true
From pois'nous herbs extracts the healing dew?

Alexander Pope, Essay on Man (ep. I, 219)

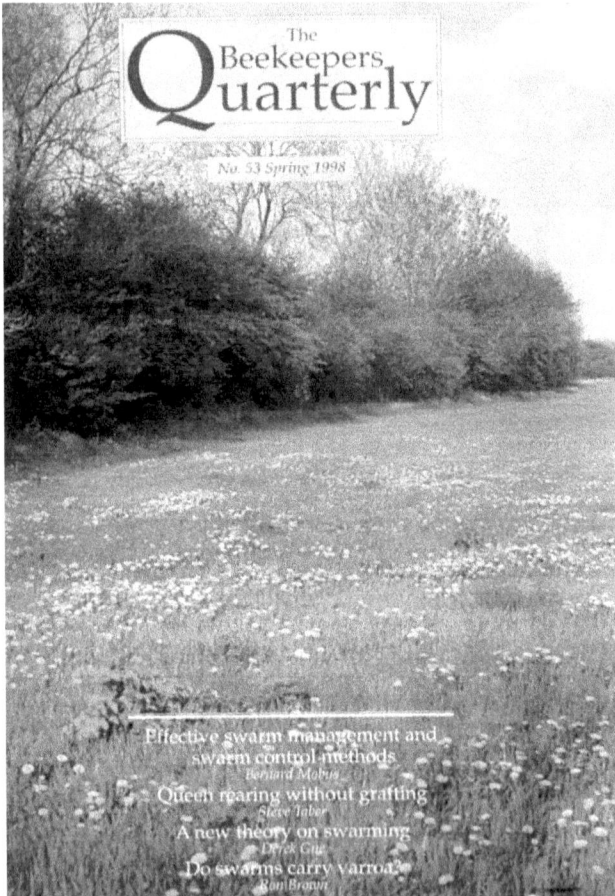

In May, when dandelions abound, the temperature is usually right for the prolonged examinations of hives. Check for varroa and diseases (especially EFB), ensure that the colonies have plenty of room and look out for swarming preparations.

DAY	MAY 2010 FORAGE	TEMP		WIND		CL'D	RAIN	1	2	3
		MIN	MAX	DIR	B.S			HIVE WEIGHT		
1										
2										
3										
4										
5										
6										
7										
8										
9										
10										
11										
12										
13										
14										
15										
16										
17										
18										
19										
20										
21										
22										
23										
24										
25										
26										
27										
28										
29										
30										
31										

MAY10

	8,SA SR 5.20, SS 8.33
1,SA SR 5.32, SS 8.21	9,SU
2,SU	10,MO
3,MO EARLY MAY BANK HOLIDAY	11,TU
4,TU	12,WE
5,WE	13,TH
6,TH	14,FR ○
7,FR	15,SA SR 5.08, SS 8.43

16,SU	24,MO
17,MO	25,TU
18,TU	26,WE
19,WE	27,TH ●
20,TH	28,FR
21,FR	29,SA SR 4.51, SS 9.03
22,SA SR 4.59, SS 8.54	30,SU
23,SU	31,MO SPRING BANK HOLIDAY

JUNE

Listen! O, listen!
Here come the hum the golden bees
Underneath full blossomed trees,
At once with glowing fruit and flowers crowned.

James Russell Lowell, The Sirens (l. 94)

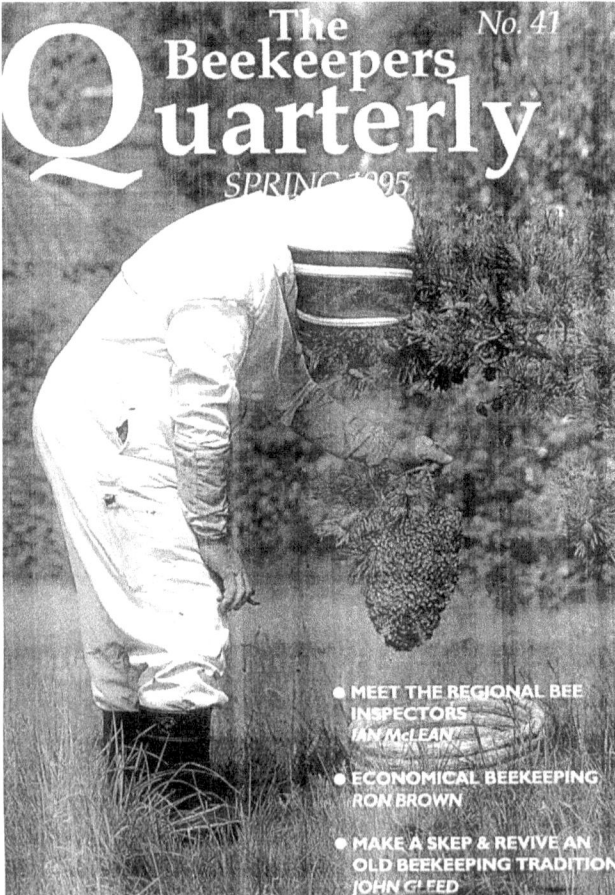

The Beekeepers Quarterly

No. 41

SPRING 1995

- MEET THE REGIONAL BEE INSPECTORS
  IAN McLEAN
- ECONOMICAL BEEKEEPING
  RON BROWN
- MAKE A SKEP & REVIVE AN OLD BEEKEEPING TRADITION
  JOHN GLEED

Most swarms usually occur this month. Have a plan beforehand of how you are going to deal with them and have all spare equipment in readiness.

DAY	JUNE 2010 FORAGE	TEMP		WIND		CL'D	RAIN	1	2	3
		MIN	MAX	DIR	B.S			HIVE WEIGHT		
1										
2										
3										
4										
5										
6										
7										
8										
9										
10										
11										
12										
13										
14										
15										
16										
17										
18										
19										
20										
21										
22										
23										
24										
25										
26										
27										
28										
29										
30										

JUN10

	8,TU
1,TU	**9,WE**
2,WE	**10,TH**
3,TH	**11,FR**
4,FR	12,SA ○ SR 4.42, SS 9.16
5,SA SR 4.45, SS 9.10	13,SU
6,SU	**14,MO**
7,MO	**15,TU**

16,WE	**24,TH**
17,TH	**25,FR**
18,FR	26,SA ● SR 4.44, SS 9.21
19,SA SR 4.42, SS 9.20	27,SU
20,SU	**28,MO**
21,MO	**29,TU**
22,TU	**30,WE**
23,WE	

JULY

For pitty, Sir, find out that Bee
Which bore my Love away
I'le seek him in your Bonnet brave,
I'le seek him in your eyes.

Robert Herrick, Mad Nan's Song

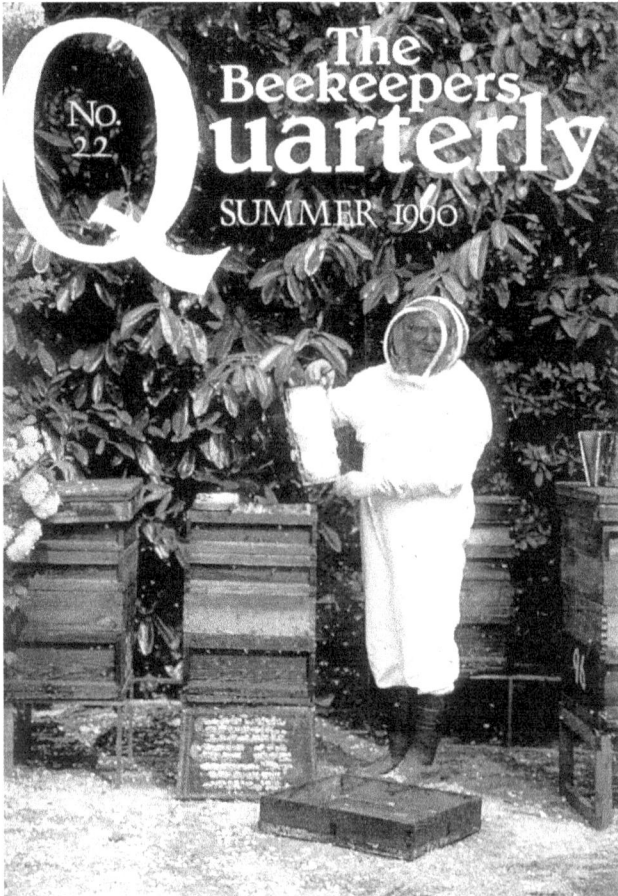

For many beekeepers most of the honey can be taken off at the end of this month. Ensure that sufficient stores are left for the bees and additionally, give them a good feed.

DAY	JULY 2010 FORAGE	TEMP		WIND		CL'D	RAIN	1	2	3
		MIN	MAX	DIR	B.S			HIVE WEIGHT		
1										
2										
3										
4										
5										
6										
7										
8										
9										
10										
11										
12										
13										
14										
15										
16										
17										
18										
19										
20										
21										
22										
23										
24										
25										
26										
27										
28										
29										
30										
31										

JUL10

	8,TH
1,TH	**9,FR**
2,FR	10,SA SR 4.54, SS 9.16
3,SA SR 4.48, SS 9.19	11,SU ○
4,SU	**12,MO**
5,MO	**13,TU**
6,TU	**14,WE**
7,WE	**15,TH**

16,FR	24,SA SR 5.11, SS 9.01
17,SA SR 5.02, SS 9.09	25,SU
18,SU	**26,MO** ⬤
19,MO	**27,TU**
20,TU	**28,WE**
21,WE	**29,TH**
22,TH	**30,FR**
23,FR	31,SA SR 5.21, SS 8.51

AUGUST

The pedigree of honey Does not concern the bee;
A clover, any time, to him Is aristocracy.

Emily Dickinson, Poems (V)

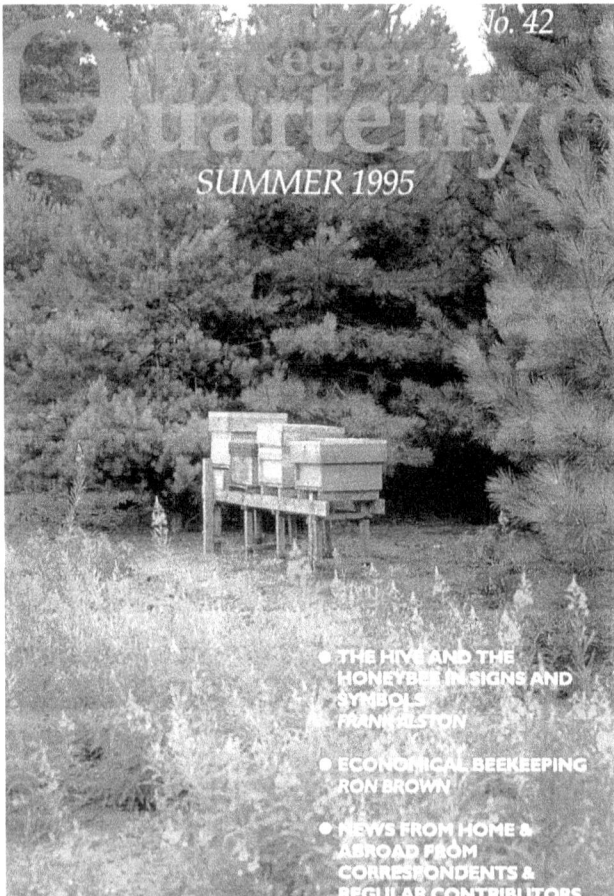

No. 42

Beekeepers Quarterly

SUMMER 1995

● THE HIVE AND THE
HONEYBEE IN SIGNS AND
SYMBOLS
FRANK ALSTON

● ECONOMICAL BEEKEEPING
RON BROWN

● NEWS FROM HOME &
ABROAD FROM
CORRESPONDENTS &
REGULAR CONTRIBUTORS

This is generally a quiet month unless bees are being taken to the heather. Feed colonies which are not being taken to other crops, then the queen will continue to lay eggs so that the colony will have a strong population of winter bees.

DAY	AUGUST 2010 FORAGE	TEMP		WIND		CL'D	RAIN	1	2	3
		MIN	MAX	DIR	B.S			HIVE WEIGHT		
1										
2										
3										
4										
5										
6										
7										
8										
9										
10										
11										
12										
13										
14										
15										
16										
17										
18										
19										
20										
21										
22										
23										
24										
25										
26										
27										
28										
29										
30										
31										

AUG10

	8,SU
1,SU	9,MO
2,MO	10,TU ○
3,TU	11,WE
4,WE	12,TH
5,TH	13,FR
6,FR	14,SA SR 5.43, SS 8.26
7,SA SR 5.32, SS 8.39	15,SU

16,MO	**24,TU** ⊙ ST BARTHOLOMEW
17,TU	**25,WE**
18,WE	**26,TH**
19,TH	**27,FR**
20,FR	28,SA SR 6.05, SS 7.57
21,SA SR 5.45, SS 8.12	29,SU
22,SU	**30,MO** SUMMER BANK HOLIDAY
23,MO	**31,TU**

SEPTEMBER

"O bees, sweet bees!" I said;
"that nearest field Is shining white with fragrant immortelles
Fly swiftly there and drain those honey wells."

Helen Hunt Jackson, My Bees.

The
Q Beekeepers
Quarterly

Feeding bees
Ken Hoare

Prisons in the Hive
Dr Francis Ratnieks

Order in the Hive
David J T Sumpter

Colonies taken to the heather should be provided with plenty of stores in the brood box as weather conditions can change rapidly on the moors. Check from time to time that they are all right and bring the colonies home as soon as the flow is over.

DAY	SEPTEMBER 2010 FORAGE	TEMP MIN	MAX	WIND DIR	B.S	CL'D	RAIN	1	2	3 HIVE WEIGHT
1										
2										
3										
4										
5										
6										
7										
8										
9										
10										
11										
12										
13										
14										
15										
16										
17										
18										
19										
20										
21										
22										
23										
24										
25										
26										
27										
28										
29										
30										

SEP10

	8,WE ○
1,WE	**9,TH**
2,TH	**10,FR**
3,FR	11,SA SR 6.27, SS 7.25
4,SA SR 6.16, SS 7.41	12,SU
5,SU	**13,MO**
6,MO	**14,TU**
7,TU	**15,WE**

16,TH	24,FR
17,FR	25,SA SR 6.50, SS 6.53
18,SA SR 6.38, SS 7.09	26,SU
19,SU	27,MO
20,MO	28,TU
21,TU	29,WE
22,WE	30,TH
23,TH ●	

OCTOBER

Look on the bee upon the wing 'mong flowers;
How brave, how bright his life! then mark, him hiv'd,
Cramp'd, cringing in his self-built, social cell,
Thus it is in the world-hive; most where men
Lie deep in cities as in drifts.

Philip James Bailey

The Beekeepers Quarterly

No. 43

AUTUMN 1995

CONSTRUCT A McBEAN HIVE BARROW
JOHN ROBINSON

GO WASSAILING AND REVIVE AN OLD TRADITION
FRANK BUCKLEY

ECONOMICAL BEEKEEPING
RON BROWN

NEWS & VIEWS FROM OUR CORRESPONDENTS AROUND THE WORLD

The National Honey Show usually takes place this year in London. Prepare exhibits well in advance of the show. Those who are not exhibiting will find the programme of lectures and workshops and the opportunity to meet hundreds of beekeepers as well as seeing what is new from the manufacturers, an unforgettable experience.

DAY	OCTOBER 2010 FORAGE	TEMP MIN	MAX	WIND DIR	B.S	CL'D	RAIN	1	2	3
								HIVE WEIGHT		
1										
2										
3										
4										
5										
6										
7										
8										
9										
10										
11										
12										
13										
14										
15										
16										
17										
18										
19										
20										
21										
22										
23										
24										
25										
26										
27										
28										
29										
30										
31										

OCT10

	8,FR
1,FR	9,SA SR 7.13, SS 6.21
2,SA SR 7.01, SS 6.37	10,SU
3,SU	**11,MO**
4,MO	**12,TU**
5,TU	**13,WE**
6,WE	**14,TH**
7,TH ○	**15,FR**

16,SA SR 7.24, SS 6.06	24,SU
17,SU	25,MO
18,MO	26,TU
19TU	27,WE
20,WE	28,TH
21,TH	29,FR
22,FR	30,SA SR 7.49, SS 5.38
23,SA ⚫ SR 7.36, SS 5.51	31,SU

NOVEMBER

His labor is a chant,
His idleness a tune;
Oh, for a bee's experience
Of clovers and of noon!

Emily Dickinson, Poems--The Bee (XV)

The
Beekeepers
Quarterly

No. 63 November 2000

Log hive Beekeeping in the Heather Forests of Ukraine
Dr Alexander Komissar
Royal Jelly Production
Gilles Fert
Greenpeace Action Against GM Crops Vindicated
Geoff Hopkinson NDB

As the leaves fall from the trees, all colonies should have been treated for varroa, be full of food, well-protected against the weather so that the beekeeper can confidently expect his colonies to come through the winter safely. From time to time check that all is well in the apiary and on mild days enjoy watching the bees as they make their flights.

DAY	NOVEMBER 2010 FORAGE	TEMP		WIND		CL'D	RAIN	1	2	3
		MIN	MAX	DIR	B.S			HIVE WEIGHT		
1										
2										
3										
4										
5										
6										
7										
8										
9										
10										
11										
12										
13										
14										
15										
16										
17										
18										
19										
20										
21										
22										
23										
24										
25										
26										
27										
28										
29										
30										

NOV10

	8,MO
1,MO	**9,TU**
2,TU	**10,WE**
3,WE	**11,TH**
4,TH	**12,FR**
5,FR	13,SA SR 7.13, SS 4.14
6,SA ○ SR 7.01, SS 4.25	14,SU
7,SU	**15,MO**

16,TU	**24,WE**
17,WE	**25,TH**
18,TH	**26,FR**
19,FR	27,SA SR 7.36, SS 3.58
20,SA SR 7.25, SS 4.05	28,SU
21,SU ●	**29,MO**
22,MO	**30,TU**
23,TU	

DECEMBER

Listen! O, listen!
Here come the hum the golden bees
Underneath full blossomed trees,
At once with glowing fruit and flowers crowned.

James Russell Lowell, The Sirens (l. 94)

With Christmas time ahead, look carefully at the catalogues of books to see which ones you would find useful or just broaden your beekeeping knowledge - better to let people know what you would like as a present should the subject come under discussion.

DAY	DECEMBER 2010 FORAGE	TEMP		WIND		CL'D	RAIN	1	2	3
		MIN	MAX	DIR	B.S			HIVE WEIGHT		
1										
2										
3										
4										
5										
6										
7										
8										
9										
10										
11										
12										
13										
14										
15										
16										
17										
18										
19										
20										
21										
22										
23										
24										
25										
26										
27										
28										
29										
30										
31										

DEC10

	8,WE
1,WE	**9,TH**
2,TH	**10,FR**
3,FR	11,SA SR 7.54, SS 3.51
4,SA SR 7.46, SS 3.53	12,SU
5,SU ○	**13,MO**
6,MO	**14,TU**
7,TU ST AMBROSE	**15,WE**

16,TH	**24,FR**
17,FR	25,SA SR 8.04, SS 3.54 CHRISTMAS DAY HOLIDAY
18,SA SR 8.01, SS 3.51	26,SU
19,SU	**27,MO**
20,MO	**28,TU** BOXING DAY HOLIDAY
21,TU ◉	**29,WE**
22,WE	**30,TH**
23,TH	

Hive/ Q NO.	Year Q Raised	Frames of Brood Autumn 2004	Combs Covered	Honey Stored- Sugar fed Kg	Combs Covered Spring 2005	Frames of Brood Spring 2005	Spring Feeding Kg	Queens Reared	Nuclei
1									
2									
3									
4									
5									
6									
7									
8									
9									
10									
11									
12									
13									
14									
15									
16									
17									
18									
19									
20									
21									
22									
23									
24									

HONEYBEE COLONIES

1								
2								
3								
4								
5								
6								
7								
8								
9								
10								
11								
12								
13								
14								
15								
16								
17								
18								
19								
20								
21								
22								
23								
24								

BEEEKEEPING RECORDS

Number	items	Est. Value £	P
	Stocks of Bees		
	Empty Hives		
	Combs - Deep - Shallow		
	Frames		
	Foundations		
	Honey Extractor		
	Honey Tanks		
	Other items		
	Honey Jars		
	Honey		

JANUARY 2011

S	M	T	W	T	F	S
						1
2	3	4	5	6	7	8
9	10	11	12	13	14	15
16	17	18	19	20	21	22
23	24	25	26	27	28	29
30	31					

FEBRUARY 2011

S	M	T	W	T	F	S
		1	2	3	4	5
6	7	8	9	10	11	12
13	14	15	16	17	18	19
20	21	22	23	24	25	26
27	28					

MARCH 2011

S	M	T	W	T	F	S
		1	2	3	4	5
6	7	8	9	10	11	12
13	14	15	16	17	18	19
20	21	22	23	24	25	26
27	28	29	30	31		

APRIL 2011

S	M	T	W	T	F	S
					1	2
3	4	5	6	7	8	9
10	11	12	13	14	15	16
17	18	19	20	21	22	23
24	25	26	27	28	29	30

MAY 2011

S	M	T	W	T	F	S
1	2	3	4	5	6	7
8	9	10	11	12	13	14
15	16	17	18	19	20	21
22	23	24	25	26	27	28
29	30	31				

JUNE 2011

S	M	T	W	T	F	S
			1	2	3	4
5	6	7	8	9	10	11
12	13	14	15	16	17	18
19	20	21	22	23	24	25
26	27	28	29	30		

JULY 2011

S	M	T	W	T	F	S
					1	2
3	4	5	6	7	8	9
10	11	12	13	14	15	16
17	18	19	20	21	22	23
24	25	26	27	28	29	30
31						

AUGUST 2011

S	M	T	W	T	F	S
	1	2	3	4	5	6
7	8	9	10	11	12	13
14	15	16	17	18	19	20
21	22	23	24	25	26	27
28	29	30	31			

SEPTEMBER 2011

S	M	T	W	T	F	S
				1	2	3
4	5	6	7	8	9	10
11	12	13	14	15	16	17
18	19	20	21	22	23	24
25	26	27	28	29	30	

OCTOBER 2011

S	M	T	W	T	F	S
						1
2	3	4	5	6	7	8
9	10	11	12	13	14	15
16	17	18	19	20	21	22
23	24	25	26	27	28	29
30	31					

NOVEMBER 2011

S	M	T	W	T	F	S
		1	2	3	4	5
6	7	8	9	10	11	12
13	14	15	16	17	18	19
20	21	22	23	24	25	26
27	28	29	30			

DECEMBER 2011

S	M	T	W	T	F	S
				1	2	3
4	5	6	7	8	9	10
11	12	13	14	15	16	17
18	19	20	21	22	23	24
25	26	27	28	29	30	31

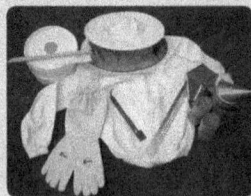

All efforts have been made to ensure the accuracy of the information in these pages. Corrections and amendments should be sent to The Editor The Beekeepers Annual, c/o Northern Bee Books, Scout Bottom Farm, Mytholmroyd, Hebden Bridge HX7 5JS

DIRECTORY, ASSOCIATIONS AND SERVICES

DIRECTORY, ASSOCIATIONS AND SERVICES

BEE MAILING

BEEKEEPING MAILING LISTS

http://www.zbee.dircon.co.uk

Beekeeping mailing list services provided by zbee.com http://www.zbee. dircon.co.uk

KENT BEEKEEPERS ASSOCIATION, THE
Name of mailing list: Kentbee-L Serving a possible membership of 400. **Support website:** http://www.kentbee.com Approximately 80 have subscribed. Providing a forum for local branch announcements and news and chat about beekeeping. **To subscribe to Kentbee-L send a message to:** mailserver@zbee.com **Subject field:** You leave this blank it doesn't matter. **In the message body write:** Subscribe Kentbee-L then send the message and await further instructions to complete the subscription process.

NATIONAL HONEY SHOW, THE
Name of mailing list: NHS The National Honey Show is held in October each year in London, the support website http://www.honeyshow.co.uk has more information and schedules, **To subscribe to NHS send a message to:** mailserver@zbee.com, **Subject field:** You leave this blank it doesn't matter., **In the message body write:** Subscribe NHS then send the message and await further instructions to complete the subscription process

BEE IMPROVEMENT & BEE BREEDERS ASSOCIATION, THE (BIBBA)
Name of mailing list: BIBBA-L, Support website http://www. bibba.com/, **To subscribe to BIBBA-L send a message to:** mailserver@zbee.com, **Subject field:** You leave this blank it doesn't matter. **In the message body write:** Subscribe BIBBA-L then send the message and await further instructions to complete the subscription process.

BEE MAILING

✉ ☎

APINET (BEEKEEPING EDUCATION EXTENSION NETWORK)
Name of mailing list: APINETL, Support website n/a, **To subscribe send a message to:** mailserver@zbee.com, **Subject field:** You leave this blank it doesn't matter.
In the message body write: Subscribe APINETL then send the message and await further instructions to complete the subscription process.

BROMLEY & SIDCUP & ORPINGTON BEEKEEPERS ASSOCIATION
Name of mailing list: BBK, **Support website:** http://www.kentbee.com/, **To subscribe to BBK send a message to:** mailserver@zbee.com, **Subject field:** You leave this blank it doesn't matter. **In the message body write:** Subscribe BBK then send the message and await further instructions to complete the subscription process.

THE BRITISH BEEKEEPERS ASOCIATION (BBKA)
Name of mailing list: BBKA, **Support website:** http://www.bbka.org.uk, Private list members only, see members area for joining details.

APIS-UK
The monthly beekeeping magazine, edited by David Cramp and sent directly to your computer. To subscribe go to www.beedata.com and click on the Apis-UK link..

BDI

SECRETARY APRIL 2009,
Roy Norris
Llys Gwyn, Cefn Mawr
Newtown
Powys SY16 3LB
01686 622217
fax, 01686 622217
roy@fulmar.
demon.co.uk

TREASURER AND
SCHEME B MANAGER
Mrs Sharon Blake
Stratton Court,
South Petherton,
Somerset TA13 5LQ
(01460) 242124
m-s.blake@overstrat-
ton.fsnet.co.uk

CLAIMS MANAGER
Bernard Diaper
57 Marfield Close,
Walmley,
Sutton Coldfield B76
1YD
0121 3133112
b.diaper@tiscali.co.uk

BEE DISEASES INSURANCE LTD

Bee Diseases Insurance provides insurance cover for individual beekeepers, association apiaries and commercial beekeepers alike, against the possibility of their bees and equipment being destroyed as a result of a Destruction Order being levied by a visiting officer from DEFRA or The Welsh Assembly Government.

The most common disease resulting in destruction is American foul brood but insurance also covers European foul brood. It should be borne in mind that colonies infected with Varroasis will be weakened and are therefore more susceptible to infection by AFB/EFB.

Scheme A provides cover for the beekeeper with a total of 39 colonies or less. Cover is obtained by being a member of a Beekeeping Association that is a member of BDI Ltd.

Scheme B provides cover for beekeepers with 40 or more colonies in total. Insurance under this Scheme is on a personal basis and further details can be obtained from the Scheme B Manager.

REMEMBER: DISEASE CAN STRIKE ANY COLONY AT ANY TIME AND IT IS SPREAD THROUGHOUT THE COUNTRY. PROTECT YOUR APIARY THROUGH B.D.I.

BEE FARMERS' ASSOCIATION OF THE UNITED KINGDOM

BEE FARMERS' ASSOCIATION

The BFA represents the professional beekeepers of the UK.

The association is the largest contract pollinator in the UK and our members are responsible for virtually all the migratory pollination. They are expected to have a good degree of competence; membership requires over 40 hives, and sponsorship by a BFA member who knows the applicant as a beekeeper. We have recently introduced a code of conduct which members are expected to observe. In addition we have a significant number of members who get some income from being bee inspectors, responsible for identifying and dealing with notifiable disease.

We have one business meeting a year which follows the Annual General Meeting in April at Stoneleigh on the same Saturday as the BBKA convention. Business is also conducted at twice-yearly regional meetings which pass items up to the main meeting for discussion and voting, and which put forward candidates for the committee.

The BFA is affiliated to the National Farmers Union and The Honey (Packers) Association with whom we work effectively in promoting ecological sensitive farming and in promoting consumer awareness through events such 'National Honey Week' and bulk sales to retail chains.

FUNCTIONS
- To monitor and to keep members informed about developments in commercial beekeeping, bee science and UK and EEC legislation.
- Liaison with Farmers, Growers, Contractors, Consumers and other organisations.
- Liaison with UK Government Departments dealing with beekeeping, medicines, and allied matters.
- Liaison and co-operation with CONBA and UK Beekeeping organisations.

CHAIRMAN, John Home
Northcote
Deppers Bridge
Southam,
Warwickshire
CV47 2SU
01926 612 322
northcote4home@
btinternet.com

VICE CHAIRMAN,
Currently vacant

TREASURER,
Mr. D. Isles
Hudnalls Apiary
The Hudnalls, St Briavels
Lydney Gloucestershire
GL15 5RT
dougisles@yahoo.co.uk

SECRETARY, J. Howat
8 Olivers Close
West Totton
Southampton SO40 8FH
02380 907850
02380 907850
john@eclipse01.
demon.co.uk

BFA

POLLINATION SEC,
Mrs M Thomas
Ballinduin Bothy
Ballinduin,
Strathtay,
Perthshire
PH9 0LP
01887 840 728
zyzythomas@
waitrose.com

BULLETIN EDITOR,
David Bancalari
Park Farm Barn
Shortthorn Road
Stratton Strawless
Norfolk
NR10 5NX
David@
Bancalari.fslife.co.uk

MEMBERSHIP SECRETARY
Gerry Fry
2, The Glade,
Waterlooville
Hants
PO7 7PD
02392 520075
gerry_fry@sky.com

- Contact with European beekeeping organisations (EPBA) and representation on the EEC Honey Working Party (COPA/COGECA) in Brussels.
- Political lobbying through MPs and Euro MPs.
- To promote the production of high quality UK honey.
- To pursue cases of misleading labeling and misrepresentation of honey.
- To provide pollination services through the National Pollination Service.
  * Active involvement in research projects, including field trials for major research projects.
  * Involvement, with others, as a stakeholder in the FERA Healthy Bees programme

FACILITIES FOR MEMBERS:

- Bi-monthly Bulletins with news and updates, notes on meetings with DEFRA, FERA, VMD, and the EEC, reports on current beekeeping problems (e.g. varroa) and commercial developments. This bulletin is available as a paper and/or an e-document
  * e-news. Frequent electronic updates on news items
- Free advertisement of members' sales and wants (including hive products, bee stocks and spare equipment).
* Regional meetings which provide for local discussion and opportunities for trading between members.
- Crop and winter loss reports.
- Free Circulation among members of UK and foreign magazines.
- Free insurance for products and third party liability (not limited to thirty hives).
- Special rates for employers liability insurance.
- Comprehensive special beefarmers insurance with the NFU.
- Pollination contracts.
- Advice from experienced members on all aspects of honey farming and commercial beekeeping; sources of equipment and sundries.
- Product directory listing specialist suppliers.
- Discounts from suppliers.
- Bulk purchase schemes.

ANNUAL CONVENTION WEEKEND

- Spring meeting for members and partners, held each March at different locations in the UK or abroad. Visits to local bee and research establishments; lectures and discussions on bee-related matters; sight seeing, and social events.

In 2010 we will be visiting the Stirling area of Scotland.

BEEKEEPING COURSES & SERVICES

PART TIME LECTURERS & FURTHER EDUCATION COURSES IN BEEKEEPING

The following may offer a range of theoretical and practical courses in beekeeping, in some cases an advisory service or a diagnostic service for adult bee diseases only may be offered.

The range of services and activities is wide and this list is not exhaustive but the following may be contacted for details of facilities in an enquirer's area.

BEDFORDSHIRE,
Gillian Sentinella
218 Old Bedford Rd
Luton, Beds
LU27 HP
01582 721814
Harry Inman
10 Constable Hill
Bedford
MK41 7LJ
01234 306554
BERKSHIRE, George Butler
• Beekeeping for Beginners/Intermediate/Advanced
• Practical Beekeeping

BERKSHIRE COLLEGE OF AGRICULTURE, Kate Malenczuk
Hall Place,
Burchetts Green
Maidenhead,
Berkshire SL6 6QR
www.bca.ac.uk
01628 824444
fax, 01628 827488
• Beekeeping for beginners
• Practical Beekeeping
• Preparing Bees for Winter
• Intermediate Beekeeping
• Taster Sessions
CHESHIRE BEEKEEPERS (STOCKPORT BRANCH)
• Introduction To Beekeeping Course,
• Practical Beekeeping, Dialstone Lane, Stockport
Details from Brian Gee
01457 867641

DEVON, Dr. Mick Street
c/o Bicton College
Budleigh Salterton
EX9 7BY
or the DBKA Education Officer at;
www.devonbeekeepers.co.uk
ESSEX, Richard Ridler
Rundle House,
High Street
Hatfield Brand Oak,
Bishop's Stortford
Hertfordshire
CM22 7HE
treasurer@ebka.org
01279 718111
07942 815753
LEEDS
For Details See YBKA

BCS

✉ ☎

NORFOLK, Paul Metcalf NDB
Easton College, Easton
Norwich NR9 8DX
SUSSEX, Business Training
Plumpton College
Ditchling Road
Plumpton, Nr Lewes
East Sussex BN7 3AE
pd@plumpton.ac.uk

STOCKPORT (see Cheshire)

WILTSHIRE,The Secretary
Melksham Beekeepers
Association
Deans End
Butts Lane
Keevil,
Trowbridge
BA14 6LZ
wickhamsoftkeevil@
btinternet.com

YBKA, Bill Cadmore,
104 Hall Lane, Horsforth
Leeds LS18 5JG
0113 216 0482
bill.cadmore@ntlworld.com
Venue:
Home Farm Rare Breeds Centre
Temple Newsam House
Garden & Estate East Leeds

BEEKEEPING EDITORS' EXCHANGE SCHEME

BEES is a self-help grouping of local, county and country beekeeping association editors, which operates principally by exchanging journals through a central address. The scheme is supported by Northern Bee Books.

BEES was founded in 1984 and for many years has been an exchange of paper copy. However, the focus has now changed to an electronic exchange, using the server of one of the participating editors.

Now fully established as part of the British and Irish beekeeping scene, the scheme brings up to date information to beekeepers throughout the British Isles.

The aims are:
- to exchange ideas for content and production methods
- to aid others by experience
- to communicate matters editorial
- to share information on national beekeeping issues
- to help and reassure those new to the task
- to give a wider readership to the best writing in beekeeping journalism

If you are an editor or potential editor and would like to know more about how we operate write to Martin Robinson.

CONTACT, Martin Robinson
The Manor House
Blackshaw Head
Hebden Bridge
West Yorks.
HX7 7JR
01422 842794
email.manorhousestudio@
talktalk.net

B.E.E.S
Helping Editors
Help Themselves

Sponsored by
NORTHERN BEE BOOKS

BEES ABROAD UK Ltd

Supporting beekeeping projects overseas

ADMINISTATOR
MRS JULES MOORE
PO BOX 2058
BRISTOL
BS35 9AF
0207 7193 7135
info@beesabroad.org.uk

Bees Abroad is a UK-registered charity (No 1108464) which was established in 1999. Its principle aim is the relief of poverty in the developing world using beekeeping and associated skills as a tool of individual, group and community empowerment for poverty alleviationand to provide sustainable income. Beekeeping is a valuable tool as it is socially and culturally acceptable for both genders across a wide age range.It can cost very little to set up a beekeeping operation, which will deliver benefits for income, education, health, environment and community. Beekeeping and its associated skills deliver access to gainful self-emplyment for poor and disadvantaged groups.   This enables them to recover social status, improve social interactions, obtain income and aquire new skills to build the confidence to represent their own interests. Bees Abroad receives a high volume of direct appeals for assistance from groups all over the world. In practice, it acheives its aims through a volunteer network of supporters, committee members and project managers.Bees Abroad takes care to ensure that its projects are sustainable and not dependent on constant external input. This is done by supporting community group initiatives, setting up village-based field extension services, running training courses for beekeeping trainers and financing local trainers' wages. All Bees Abroad projects are designed to become self-financing after a defines time period, usually 2-3 years, but sometimes longer. Its first two projects in Nepal and Cameroon now employ 42 beekeeper trainers and involve many more. It currently has projects either runnung or seeking funding in Malawi, Kenya, Ghana, Nepal, Uganda and Nigeria.

Our committee is almost entirely run by volunteers, who are all beekeepers. Volunteers and members currently undertake all activities, including fundraising, though a part-time administrator is employed for one day a week. We also arrange Beekeeping Holidays to variety of locations, including Chile, Cameroon and Kenya.
For more details of what we do and how you can help, you can contact Mrs Jules Moore the Administrator, Bees Abroad. Membership costs £15.00 per annum.

BFD

BEES FOR DEVELOPMENT TRUST

(UK Registered Charity 1078803)

www.beesfordevelopment.org

CONTACT, Dr Nicola Bradbear
Bees for Development
PO Box 105, Monmouth,
NP25 9AA
Tel 016007 13648

E-mail. info@
beesfordevelopment.org
Web www.
beesfordevelopment.org

PLEASE SUPPORT BEES FOR DEVELOPMENT
Ways you can help

☐ Subscribe to Bees for Development Journal
☐ Sponsor a subscription and encourage your Association to do likewise
☐ Give a donation
☐ Join one of our Safaris
☐ Buy our special labels and tamper proof seals for your honey jars and bee products
☐ Buy your bee reading and viewing from us

Bees for Development works to provide information to beekeepers in developing countries where reliable apicultural information is hard to find. We advocate beekeeping as an effective way for people to create income from natural resources without damaging them. We respond to 4,000 enquiries that arrive by e-mail and post from beekeepers in developing countries each year.

Our work

Bees for Development Journal: Enjoyed by readers in over 100 countries, our Journal keeps everyone in our network in touch. 95% of recipients cannot afford to pay a subscription and therefore we seek funding to sponsor them. We are assisted in this significant task by our charity Bees for Development Trust.

Project management: current examples - Bees, people and forest biodiversity in South India; Increasing honey trade in Uganda; Investigating beekeeping potential to assist subsistence farmers in southern Sudan.

Expert advice: We assist enquirers from developing countries without charging a fee. For those living elsewhere we make a nominal charge.

Beekeepers' Safaris: Friendly holidays run in co-operation with our overseas partners.

Beekeeping books, videos, CDs and posters: see our comprehensive web store.

Training courses, study tours and symposia and presentations about our work.

BRITISH BEEKEEPERS' ASSOCIATION www.bbka.org.uk

COMMITTEES OF THE EXECUTIVE AND SECRETARIES

FINANCE COMMITTEE
The Finance Committee reviews and agrees budgets and deals with issues relating to insurance, investments and setting the proposals for capitation etc. It acts as a co-ordinator for all external fund raising.

EDUCATION & HUSBANDRY
The Education & Husbandry Committee develops practical guidance on beekeeping, produces advisory leaflets on husbandry topics, liaises with the Examination Board to develop training material and seminars to support Area Association tutors.

EXAMINATION BOARD
Sec,Mrs Val Francis, 39 Beevor Lane, Gawber, Barnsley,S75 2RP, (01226) 286 341
The Examination Board is responsible for the examinations framework of the BBKA and for setting written and practical examinations in support of the BBKA's desire to educate and set standards for beekeepers. The Examination Board is also responsible for the management of the correspondence courses to help beekeepers to train for BBKA examinations and qualifications.

The Publicity and Promotions Committee seeks ways to promote bees and beekeeping at both local and national level. It monitors media coverage and ensures that BBKA contributes to any relevant debate.

GENERAL SECRETARY
Mike Harris
National Beekeeping Centre
NAC, Stoneleigh Park
Warwickshire CV8 2LG
024 7669 6679
Fax: 024 7669 0682
gereralsecretary@
britishbeekeepers.com

BBKA HEADQUARTERS
National Beekeeping Centre
Stoneleigh Park, Stoneleigh
Warks CV8 2LG
0240 7669 6679
Fax: 024 7669 0682
Office hours 9.00am–14.30
Monday - Friday (inclusive)
Telephone answering service outside office hours
bbka@britishbeekeepers.com

Letitia Hammon,
Office Administrator

EXAMINATIONS BOARD SEC
Mrs Val Francis
39 Beevor Lane
Gawber
Barnsley S75 2RP
01226 286 341
valfrancis@blueyonder.co.uk

BBKA

EXECUTIVE COMMITTEE

PRESIDENT
TIM LOVETT
The Ruthings, 45 FoleyRd
Claygate, Esher
Surrey KT10 0LU
tjl@dermapharm.co.uk

VICE CHAIRMAN
Martin Smith,
137, Blaguegate Lane,
Skelmersdale, WN8 8TX
ormskirk-beekeepers@
hotmail.com

TREASURER
Miss A West
Sunnybank, Mells
Somerset BA11 3PE

MEMBERS

Ms P. Allen
8, Frank's Cottages
St. Mary's Lane
Upminster, RM14 3NU
pat.allen@btconnect.com

David Aston
38,Main St,Wressle,
Nr. Selby, Yorks.YO8 7ET
01757 638 758
daston49@hotmail.com

TECHNICAL

The Technical Committee monitors technical developments and assesses their potential impact on bees and beekeeping.

SUBSCRIPTIONS AND MEMBERSHIP FEES

Individual membership fees are now £18 for an overseas member or £33 per annum for UK members.

EXAMINATIONS

The Examination Board of the BBKA performs a national function, providing a structured range of examinations fulfilling the needs of all beekeepers. All matters concerning examinations, except for the correspondence course, should be addressed to the Examination Secretary.

CORRESPONDENCE COURSES

Courses to prepare candidates for the Basic Examination, and Modular Examinations are available. Details from the Courses Secretary, C.J. Utting, Codden, Golf Links Road, Westward Ho!, Bideford, Devon, EX39 1HH, 01237 474500.

LEGAL ADVICE

The Legal Adviser to the BBKA may be able to help Local Associations with legal problems to a limited extent. Contact through the General Secretary, Mike Harris, BBKA, Stoneleigh Park, Kenilworth, CV8 2LG.

SPRAY PROBLEMS

Help and advice for members who have suffered losses from poisonous sprays may be obtained from the Technical Committee Secretary.

EVENTS

The various gatherings of beekeepers continue to be a feature of BBKA's many functions and provide a vital service for the dissemination of knowledge and the drawing together of members.

122

The Spring Convention at Stoneleigh, combined with the comprehensive features of the Bee Fair, is now a firmly established event. From time to time, day or weekend courses are held on special subjects. The BBKA has stands featuring bees and promoting beekeeping at a number of national agricultural and garden shows throughout the year.

INSURANCE

Every Individual Member and every, Area Association and its Branches/Divisions is indemnified against claims for Public Liability and Product Liability to a limit of £5 million. The beekeeper must bear the first £250 of each and every claim.

Two other types of insurance are available to beekeepers:

1 The "All Risks" which covers loss of or damage to hives and equipment

2 The BBKA Combined Insurance Scheme for Member Associations, which covers various activities of associations.

Further details can be obtained from the BBKA Treasurer.

PUBLICATIONS

• BBKA Year Book contains detailed information about BBKA including the Annual Report of the Executive and other committees and the Annual Accounts. Copies can be obtained from Headquarters for £2.00 + 9" x 6" s.a.e.

• BBKA News is issued six times a year, free to all members of BBKA. The Editor/Advertising Manager is Mrs. S. Blake, Stratton Court, Over Stratton, South Petherton, Somerset TA13 5LQ.

• Directory of Lecturers & Demonstrators is included in the Year Book.

ITEMS FOR SALE

The Association's range can be bought at several of the major national events. Mail order enquiries should be addressed to The General Secretary, BBKA, Stoneleigh-Park, Stoneleigh, Kenilworth, CU8 2LG

Michael Badger MBE MA
Kara,,14 Thorn Lane
Roundhay, Leeds
LS8 1NN
buzz.buzz@ntlworld.com

Chris Deaves
12 Chatsworth Crescent
Houndslow TW3 2PB
c-deaves@compuserve.com

Brian P. Dennis
50 Station Rd, Cogen Hoe
Northamptonshire NN7 1LU
herebebees@tiscali.co.uk

Pam Hunter
Burnthouse,Burnthouse Lane,
Cowfold, Horsham
W Sussex RH13 8DH
pamhunter@
burnthouse.org.uk

Roger Patterson
Kenton, Norwich Road
Barnham Broom, NR9 4BU
paul.metcalfe@talk21.com

Dr Stephen Palmer
3 Hayes Lane, Slinford,
Sussex, RH13 0SQ
r.patterson@
pattersonpressings.co.uk

Brian Ripley
6 Chibburn Court,
Widdrington Station, Morpeth
Northumberland NE61 5QT
brian.ripley@feeserve.com

Bob Robinson
Heath Cottage, Stairs Hill
Liss,Hampshire GU33 6HR
bobr@skylon.co.uk

Martin Smith
137 Blaguegate Lane
Skelmersdale, WN8 8TX
ormskirk-beekeepers@
hotmail.com

BBKA

BBKA SLIDES OFFICER, R. Hoskins
Larkfield, Covingham
Swindon, Wilts, SN3 5AD
(01793) 525364

The main items are:

• Leaflets – a number of reasonably priced leaflets on beekeeping matters.

• Show material – a range of Prize Cards, Class Cards, Labels and specimen Show Rules, Honey Grading Filters and Medals.

• Hive Plans – detailed plans for the construction of Modified National, Smith, WBC and Langstroth hives and the Sundown Floor.

• Other items – Honeybee Anatomy Transparencies, Badges, Brooches, Ties.

AUDIO-VISUAL AIDS LIBRARY

A wide selection of video cassettes, projection slides and sound cassettes on beekeeping and conservation generally is available, including two videos on varroa.

Requests for video and sound cassettes, projection and microscope slides should be made to BBKA Slides Officer, R. Hoskins, 10 Larksfield, Covingham Park, Swindon, Wilts, SN3 5AD, 01793 525364.

Catalogues of available material are available for 75p on receipt of a 9" x 6" s.a.e. New Material is reviewed by the librarian who welcomes enquiries, suggestions and donations of items to improve the service.

BBKA

AREA ASSOCIATION SECRETARIES

AVON, Ms Julie Young
1, Church Cottages
Abson Rd
Abson, Bristol
BS30 5TT
0117 937 2156
BERKSHIRE, Martin Moore,
19 Armour Hill
Tilehurst
READING
RG31 6JP
01189677386
07729620286
secretary.berksbees@
uwclub.net
BOURNEMOUTH
Mr A Curry
40 Lacy Drive,
Wimbourne, BW21 1DG
01202 840993
andrew@curry@virgin.net
BUCKS, Mr Richard Simpson
Delcroft
Stylecroft Road
Chalfont St Giles
HP8 4HX
01494 875105
CAMBRIDGESHIRE
Mrs Beryl Flack
21 Denny end Rd
Waterbeach,
Cambridge, CB25 9PB
01223 860 960
beryl.bee@ntlworld.com
CHESHIRE, M.F. Haynes
98, Gatley Road, Gatley,
Cheadle, Cheshire SK8 4AB
0161 491 2382
thesecretary@cheshire-bka.
co.uk

CHESTERFIELD, Robin Bagnall
21 Ramper Avenue,
Clowne, Chesterfield
Derbyshire S43 4UD
01246 570545
ancient.mariner74-79@
virgin.net
CORNWALL, Julia Cooper
Whistow Farm, Lanlivery,
Bodmin, PL30 5DE
01208 872865
julia.i.cooper@btinternet.com
CORNWALL WEST
Mrs Berenice Robbins
7 Warwick Avenue,
Illogan, Redruth
Cornwall, TR16 4DZ
01209 842 998
CUMBRIA, Stephen C Barnes
8 Albemarle Street
Cockermouth
Cumbria CA13 0BG
01900 824872
e-mail, borderer@aol.com
DERBYSHIRE, M J Cross
Harlestone, Beggarswell
Wood, Ambergate
Derbyshire DE56 2HF
01773 852772
crosssk@btinternet.com
DEVON, Andrew Kyle
62 Bicton Street,
Exmouth EX8 2RU
01395 263509
andrewkyle@tiscali.co.uk
DORSET, Mrs Ruth Homer
5, Malters Cottage,
Litton Cheney,
Dorchester DT2 9AE
beekeepers@hotmail.com

DOVER & DISTRICT
Mrs Maggie Harrowell
4 Harton Cottages, Ashley,
Dover, CT15 5HS
01304 821208
the.harrowells@btinternet.com
DURHAM, John Metson
7 Sidegate, Durham City,
Durham
0191 384 5170
ESSEX, Mrs Pat Allen
8 Frank's Cottages
St Mary's Lane
Upminster RM14 3NU
01708 220897
pat.allen@btconnect.com
GLOUCESTERSHIRE
Mrs Victoria Logue
Whitehall Farmhouse
Sevenhampton
Cheltenham,Glos' GL54 5TL
01242 820772
Mrs J Bromley
Ty Hir, Monmouth Road
Raglan, Usk. NP15 2ET
01291 690331
bromleyjan@hotmail.com
HAMPSHIRE, Mrs P Barker
Brookdean, Hillbrow
Liss, Hampshire GU33 7PT
01730 895368
H'GATE & RIPON
Mr Frank Ward
19 High Street
Starbeck, Harrogate
HG2 7NS
01423 880266

BBKA

HEREFORDSHIRE
Mrs. Wendy Cummins
Brook Cottage
Whitbourne
Worcsestershire WR6 5RT
01886 821485
jerryandwendy@btinternet.com

HERTFORDSHIRE
Luke Adams
53 Park Street Lane
Park Street
St. Albans
Hertfordshire AL2 2JA
01442 843 779
luke.skywalker@virgin.net

HUNTINGDON,
Nick Steiger
Bull Cottage, Main Street,
Upton, Huntingdon, Cambs,
PE28 5YB
01480 891935
n.steiger@btinternet.com

ISLE OF MAN,
Judith Cain
Anchorage Guest House
Athol Park, Port Erin
Isle of Man IM9 6EX
01624 832355

ISLE OF WIGHT,
Mrs. Mary Case
Limerstone Farm
Limerstone,
Newport
Isle of White PO404AB
01983 759510

KENDAL &
SOUTH WESTMORLAND
Roger Blocksidge
Castle Garden Cottage
Aynam Road, Kendal
Cumbria LA9 7DE
01539 734436
tinky_winky@hotmail.com

KENT, John D. Hendrie
26 Coldharbour Lane
Hildenborough, Tonbridge
Kent TN11 9JT
01732 833894
jdh@bbka.freeserve.co.uk

LANCASHIRE & NORTH WEST
Martin Smith
137 Blaguegate Lane,
Lathom
Skelmersdale
Wigan WN8 8TX
05601 484388
ormskirk_beekeepers@
hotmail.com

LINCOLNSHIRE
Mrs. Celia Smith
Brookfield, Moor Town Road,
Nettleton LN7 6HX
01472 851165

LONDON
Nikki Vane
601 Alaska, 61 Grange Road
London SE1 3BB
07909 964986
sec@lbka.org.uk

LUDLOW & DIST
Andy M Vanderbrook
The Old Forge
Baveney Wood
Cleobury Mortimer
Kidderminster
DY14 8JD
01299 841379
andy.vanderhook@
care4free.net

MANCH. & DIST, Mrs. M. Bohme
54 Dunster Drive, Flixton
Manchester M41 3WR
0161 747 7292

MEDWAY Mrs. M. Pines
26 Lapwing Road
Isle of Grain, Rochester
ME3 0EB
01634 272252

MIDDLESEX, Mrs. J.V. Telfer
Midwood House
Elm Park Road
Pinner HA5 3LH
020 8868 3494
jvtelfer@hotmail.com

MOLE APIARY CLUB,
Ms Angela Hume
The Cottage
Farewell Lane
West Horsley, Surrey
KT24 6DE
014832 83154

NEWCASTLE & DISTRICT,
Mr D Varty
Cragside, Dipton
Stan DH9 9EL
01207 570229

NORFOLK, Mrs H Coppwaite
1 The Maltings, Millgate
Aylsham, Norwich
NR11 6GX
01263 734682

NORFOLK WEST & KINGS LYNN
Mrs Irene Laws
16 Pine Road,
South Wootton
King's Lynn PE30 3JP
01553 671312

NORTHAMPTONSHIRE
Mrs Margaret Lawson
1 The Knoll
Grendon
Northampton NN7 1JG
01933 665017

NORTHUMBERLAND
Mr Ben Hopkinson
11 Watershaugh Rd
Warkworth, Northumberland
NE65 0TT
01665 714213
benhopkinson2436@waitrose.com

NOTTINGHAMSHIRE
M. Jordan
29 Crow Park Avenue
Sutton on Trent
Nr Newark NG23 6QG
(01636) 821613
msjordan@tiscali.co.uk

OXFORDSHIRE, Mrs Sally Moyes
The Grange, 31 Acre End St
Eynsham, Oxon OX29 4PF
01865 880 288
sallymoyes@ntlworld.com

PETERBOROUGH & DISTRICT
P George Newton
65 Queen Street, Yaxley
Peterborough PE7 7JE
01733 243349

SEDBURGH
Jane Callus-Whitton
Harren House, Woodman
Lane, Cowan Bridge,
Carnforth, LA6 2HT
01524 272004

SHROPSHIRE
Mrs Penny Carkeet-James
Upper Dumble Holes
Westbury
Shrewsbury SY5 9HE
01743 791081

SHROPSHIRE NORTH
Mrs Jo Schup
Fields Farm, Malt Kiln Lane
Dobsons Bridge,
Whixall SY13 2QL
01948 720731

SOMERSET,
Mrs S Perkins
Tengore House,
Tengore Lane, Langport
Somerset TA10 9JL
01458 250095
bernieperkns.tengor@tiscali.co.uk

STAFFORDSHIRE NORTH
Janey Hayward
90 Ostler's Lane
Cheddleton ST13 7HS
01538 361048

STAFFORDSHIRE SOUTH
Tony Burton
96 Weeping Cross, Stafford,
Staffordshire ST17 0DH
01784 663 340
tony@loweaves.fsnet.co.uk

STRATFORD-ON-AVON
Michael Osborne
Oak Lodge, King's Lane
Snitterfield
Stratford-upon-Avon
Warwickshire CV37 0RB
01789 731745
mjroosborne@btinternet.com

SUFFOLK,
Ian McQueen
643 Foxhall Road
Ipswich IP3 8NE
01473 420187
jackie.mcqueen@ntlworld.com

SURREY, Mrs Sandra Rickwood
19 Kenwood Drive,
Walton-on-Thames
Surrey. KT12 5AU
01932 244 326
rickwoodbka@googlemail.com

SUSSEX, Mrs R H M Champion
45 Ridgeway, Hurst Green
Etchingham TN19 7PJ
01580 860379

SUSSEX WEST,
Mr John Glover
Fletchings Hollow
Vicarage Hill, Loxwood,
West Sussex RH14 0RJ
01403 751 899
glover.fletchershollow@googlemail.com

THANET,
Mrs R Pearce
Summerfield Cottage
Summerfield
Woodnesborough
Nr Sandwich CT13 0EW
01304 614789

TWICKENHAM & THAMES VALLEY
Mrs Sarah Crofton
11 Wellesley Avenue
London TW3 2PB
0208 222 8216

WARWICKSHIRE,
Carolyn Mann
4 Woodbine Street
Leamington Spa
Warwickshire
CV32 5BG
01926 831672
secretary@warwickshirebeekeepers.org.uk

WILTSHIRE,
Ruth Woodhouse
Sandridge Tower
Bromham
Devizes
SN15 2JN
01225 705382
sandridgetower@aol.com

BBKA

WORCESTERSHIRE
Mrs Ursula Brandwood
10 Monnow Close
Droitwich Spa
Worcester
WR9 8TF
01905 772070
ursula@brandwoodu.
freeserve.co.uk

WYE VALLEY, Mrs S Wenczek
Hopleys, Bearwood
Leominster HR6 8EQ
01544 388302
YORKSHIRE, Brian Latham
111 Woodland Road
Whitkirk, Leeds
LS15 7DN
0113 264 3436

ASSOCIATION EXAMINATION SECRETARIES

AVON, Position Vacant
Please contact
Hon. General Secretary
Julie Young
01179 372 156
BERKSHIRE,
Mrs Rosemary Bayliss
Norbury, Coppid Beech Hill,
Binfield, Berkshire.
RG42 4BS
01344 421747
BOURNEMOUTH, Mrs. M. Davies
80 Leybourne Avenue
Ensbury Park
Bournemouth
Dorset BH10 6HE
01202 526077

BUCKS, John Chudley
Orchard Lea, Oxford Street
Lea Common
Great Missenden HP16 9JT
01494 837544
jlchudley@tiscali.co.uk
CHESHIRE, S.L. Kidman
1 Melloncroft Drive
West Kiby
Wirral CH48 2JA
(0151) 625 9544
CORNWALL
Mrs. Susan Malcolm
Fig Tree, 333 New Road
Saltash, Cornwall
PL12 6HL
01752 845496

DEVON, Roger Lacey
Gatchell House
Toadpit Lane, Ottery St Mary
Devon EX11 1TR
01404 811733
devonbees@pobox.com
DORSET, J. G. Bishop
72 Alexandra Road
Bridport DT6 5AL
01308 425479
DURHAM, G. Eames
23 Lancashire Drive
Belmont, Durham,
DH1 2DE
01913 845220
george.eames@durham.ac.uk

ESSEX, Pat Allan
8, Frank's Cottages
St. Mary's Lane
Upminster, RM14 3NU
pat.allen@btconnect.com

GLOUCESTERSHIRE
Bernard Danvers
120a Ruspidge Road
Cinderford,
Glocestershire
GL143AG
01594 825063

GWENT, Mrs J Bromley
Ty Hir, Monmouth Road
Raglan, Usk. NP15 2ET
01291 690331
bromleyjan@hotmail.com

HAMPSHIRE, Mrs Peggy Mason
37 Springford Crescent
Lordswood,
SO16 5LF
023 8077 7705

H'GATE & RIPON, M.J.M. Annett
3 Rossett Drive, Harrogate
HG2 9NS (01423) 872715

HEREFORDSHIRE, Len J. Dixon
The Square, Titley,
Kington
Herefordshire HR5 3RG
01544 230884
beeline2ljd@yahoo.co.uk

HERTFORDSHIRE, R. E. A. Dartington
15 Benslow Lane
Hitchin SG4 9RE
01462 450707
gray.dartington@dial.pipex.com

ISLE OF WIGHT, Mrs M. Case
Limerstone Farm,
Limerstone, Newport,
Isle of Wight, PO30 4AB
01983 740223
gcase90337@aol.com

KENT, P. F. W. Hutton
22 Good Station Road
Tunbridge Wells,
TN1 2DB
01892 530688

LANCASHIRE & NW
Edward Hill
3 Sandy Lane, Aughton
Ormskirk
L39 6SL
01695 423137

LEICESTERSHIRE & RUTLAND
Brian Cramp
2 Woodland Drive, Groby
Leicester
LE6 0BQ
01162 876879

LINCOLNSHIRE, R. J. B. Hickling
Linden Lea, Sandbraes
Lane, Caistor, LN7 6SB
01472 851473

MIDDLESEX
Mrs Jo V Telfer
Midwood House
Elm Park Road, Pinner
Middlesex HA5 3LH
020 8868 3494
e-mail, jvtelfer@hotmail.com

NOTTINGHAMSHIRE
Dr Glyn D Flowerdew
Knight Cross Cottage
Newstead Abbey Park
Ravenshead
Nottinghamshire NG15 8GE
01623 792812

OXFORDSHIRE, Terry. Thomas
4 Kirk Close
Oxford, OX2 8JN
01865 558679

PETERBOROUGH, P. G .Newton
65 Queen Street, Yaxley
Peterborough PE7 3JE
01733 243349

SHROPSHIRE NORTH
Paul Curtis
1 Hammer Close
Overton-on-Dee, Wrexham
Clwyd LL13 0LD0
01691 624296

SOMERSET, Mrs S Perkins
Tengore House,
Tengore Lane, Langport
Somerset TA10 9JL
(01458) 250095

STAFFS.Nth Dr. Nick C Mawby
Glenwood, Wood Lane
Longsdon,
Stoke on Trent ST9 9QB
01538 387506
info@northstaffsbees.org.uk

STAFFS. SOUTH
Tony Burton
96 Weeping Cross, Stafford,
Staffordshire. ST9 9QB
01538 399322

SUFFOLK, Jeremy Quinlan
The Old Rectory
Dallinghoo, Woodbridge
Suffolk IP13 0LA
01473 737700

SURREY, Mrs. A. Gill
143 Smallfield Road
Horley, RH6 9LR
01293 784161

SUSSEX, Nigel Champion
45 Ridgeway,
Hurst Green
Etchingham
East Sussex TN19 7PJ
01580 860379

SUSSEX WEST
Mrs A. S. Gibson-Poole
Mont Dore, West Hill
High Salvington
Worthing, BN13 3BZ
01903 260914

BBKA

✉ ☎

TWICKENHAM, Chris Deaves
12 Chatsworth Crescent
Hounslow,
Middlesex
TW3 2PB
0208 5682869
e-mail,
c-deavs@compuserve.com

WARWICKSHIRE, P.D. Lishman
Aston Farm House
Newtown Lane
Shustoke, ColeshillB46 2SD
01676 540411

WILTSHIRE, John Troke
The Lythe
Hop Gardens
Whiteparish, Salisbury,
Wiltshire SP5 2SS
01373 822892

WORCHESTERSHIRE, D.P. Friel
17 Tennal Rd, Harborne
Birmingham, B32 2JD
0121 427 1211

YORKSHIRE, D. R. Gue
87 Grove Park
Beverley, HU17 9JU
01482 881288

Where Associations have no Examinations Secretary the Association Secretary deals with examinations. To help future candidates it is suggested that Associations without an Examination Secretary appoint one. Associations are responsible for arranging a suitable room for the written examinations and recommending an invigilator.

If you live in an area without a nominated Exam Secretary, you should contact Mrs Val Frances, 39 Beevor Lane, Gawber, Barnsley, S75 2RP   Tel 01226 286341. e-mail, valfrances@blueyonder.co.uk

HOLDERS OF THE BBKA SENIOR JUDGES CERTIFICATE

ASHLEY, Mr. T. E.
Meadow Cottage
Elton Lane, Winterley
Sandbach
Cheshire CW11 4TN

BADGER, M.J , MBE
14 Thorn Lane
Leeds, LS8 1NN

BLACKBURN, Mrs. H.M
15 Highdown Hill Road
Emmer Green
Reading RG4 8QR

BROWN, Mrs. V
20 Swains Lane
Flackwell Heath HP10 9PU

BUCKLE, M.J
The Little House
Newton Blossomville
Bedford MK43 8AS

CAPENER, Rev. H.F.
1 Baldric Road
Folkestone CT20 2NR

COLLINS, G.M. , NDB
72 Tatenhill Gardens
Doncaster DN4 6TL

COOPER, Miss R.M
10 Gaskells End
Tokers Green
Reading RG4 9EW

DANIELS, D.H
Mellifera, 14 Frenches Mead
Billingshurst RH14 9LF

DAVIES, Mrs. M
80 Leybourne Avenue
Ensbury Park
Bournemouth BH10 6HE

DIAPER, B
57 Marfield Close, Walmley
Sutton Coldfield B76 1YD

DICKSON, Ms. F
Didlington Manor
Didlington, Thetford
Norfolk IP26 5AT

DUFFIN, J.M
Upper Hurst
Salisbury Road, Blashford
Ringwood
Hampshire BH24 3PB

DUGGAN, R.M
Redstone Wood Cottage
Philanthropic Lane
Redhill RH1 4DF

FIELDING, L.G
Linley, Station Road
Lichfield WS13 6HZ

MacGIOLLA COSA, M.C.
Glengarra Wood, Burncourt
Cahir, Co. Tipperary
Republic of Ireland

McCORMICK, E.
14 Akers Lane, Eccleston St.
Helens, Lancs WA10 4QL

MOXON, G
9 Savery Street
Southcoates Lane
Hull HU9 3BG

ORTON J
Occupation Road, Sibson
Nuneaton CV13 6LD

ROUNCE J.N , NDB
4 Scarborough Road
Great Walsingham
NR22 6AB

SALTER T.A , MBE
44 Edward Road, Clevedon
North Somerset BS21 7DT

SYMES, C.J
189 Marlow Bottom Road
Marlow SL7 3PL

TAYLOR, A.J
The Old Pyke Cottage
Hethelpit Cross, Staunton
GL19 3QJ

VICKERY, R.G.L
Ponderosa, Verwood Road
Three Legged Cross
Wimborne BH21 6RN

WILLIAMS, M
Tincurry, Cahir,
Co Tipperary, Eire

YOUNG, M
Mileaway, Carnreagh
Hillsborough,
Northern Island BT26 6LJ

BIBBA

BEE IMPROVEMENT & BEE BREEDERS' ASSOCIATION

www.bibba.com

SECRETARY AND MEMBERSHIP SECRETARY
Brian Dennis
50 Station Road,
Cogenhoe
Northants NN7 1LU
01604 890117
membership@bibba.com

BIBBA is an organisation devoted to encouraging beekeepers to breed native bees. The bee more suited to our environmental circumstances than other sub species. BIBBA's aims are publicised through books, workshops, lectures and conferences.

BIBBA also co-operates with worldwide Beekeeping and breeding groups interested in conserving and improving their own native bees.

SALES SECRETARY,
John Hendrie
26 Coldharbour Lane
Hildenborough
Tonbridge
Kent
TN11 9JT
sales@bibba.com

Breeding techniques advocated include:

• Assessment of colonies by observation, recording certain criteria on standard record cards.
• Determination and purity of sub species by measurement of morphometric characters and mitrochondial DNA.
• Use of mini nucs for the mating of queens economically

BIBBA Publications include:

• The Honeybees of the British Isles by Beowulf Cooper
• Breeding Techniques and Selection for Breeding of the Honeybee by Prof. F. Ruttner
• The Dark European Honey Bee by Prof. F. Ruttner, Rev. Eric Milner and John Dews
• Breeding Better Bees using Simple Modern Methods by John E. Dews and Rev. Eric Milner
• Better Beginnings for Beekeepers by Adrian Waring - second edition.

BIBBA encourages the formation of Bee Breeding Groups, and the sharing of knowledge between groups by the provision of genetic material.
Look out for Queen Rearing events in the bee press and on www.bibba.com.

THE C.B. DENNIS BRITISH
BEEKEEPERS' RESEARCH TRUST

REGISTERED CHARITY NO. 328685

Aims

This Charitable Trust was established in 1990 through the generosity of Mr. C.B. Dennis. It aims to use the interest from the capital investment to support British research projects that are likely to benefit beekeeping in the relatively short term, giving some priority to work on bee diseases.

Awards

The Trust is an independent body making awards to institutions or individuals on the basis of scientific merit of submitted proposals and perceived benefit to British beekeeping. Since the foundation of the Trust more than thirty awards in diverse areas of bee research have been made. Particular encouragement is given to young scientists through travel bursaries to enable students or researchers at the start of their careers to attend national or international meetings to present their work. A three year studentship supervised by Dr Dave Goulson at the University of Stirling has now been completed. This examined the population structure of rare and declining bumble bee species with a view to answering some key questions about their conservation. Applications for further studentships are invited.

Further details of the work of the Trust, application forms for research project funding and guidance notes for applicants are available on request from the Secretary.

Donations

The Trust is pleased to acknowledge the loyal support it already receives from several local beekeeping associations and many individuals. All donations, however small, will be added to the invested capital and bee research in Britain will benefit from the income in perpetuity. Supporting the Trust will ensure that sufficient income is generated to initiate the research that beekeepers would like to see undertaken.

All donations, correspondence and requests for grant application forms should be sent to the secretary.sufficient income is generated to initiate the research that beekeepers would like to see undertaken.

PLEASE THINK ABOUT THIS AND HELP IF YOU CAN
All donations and correspondence should be sent to the secretary

CABK

✉ ☎

THE CENTRAL ASSOCIATION OF BEEKEEPERS

www.cabk.org.uk

SECRETARY, Pat Allen
8 Frank's Cottages
St Mary's Lane
Upminster, RM14 3NU

PRESIDENT, Prof. R.S. Pickard
Consumer's Association
2 Marylebone Rd
London, NW1 4DF

TREASURER, John Hendrie
26 Coldharbour Lane
Hildeborough
Tonbridge, TN11 9JT

PROGRAMME SECRETARY
Pam Hunter
Burnthouse
Burnthouse Lane
Cowfold, Horsham
RH13 8DH

EDITOR, Pat Allen
8, Frank's Cottages
St. Mary's Lane
Upminster, RM14 3NU

SALES AND DISTRIBUTION,
Margaret Thomas
The Battinbuin Bothy
Battinbuin, Strathtay,
Pitlochy, PH9 0LP

The Central Association of Beekeepers in its present form dates from the time of the reorganisation of the British Beekeepers' Association in 1945. The BBKA was originally made up of private members only. However as County Associations were formed they applied for affiliation and were later permitted to send delegates to meetings of the Central Association, as the private members were then known. This arrangement became unsatisfactory as the voting power of the Central Association greatly outnumbered that of the County Associations and so in 1945 a new Constitution was drawn up whereby the Council comprised Delegates from the Counties and Specialist Member Associations. The private members then formed themselves into a Specialist Member Association with the designation 'The Central Association of the British Beekeepers' Association'; this was later shortened to its present style.

The Association was able to devote itself to its own particular aims, to promote interest in current thought and findings about beekeeping and aspects of entomology related to honey-bees and other social insects. Lectures given by scientists and other specialists are arranged, printed and circulated to members, as has been done since 1879.

An annual Spring Conference is held in London and an Autumn Conference in the Midlands. In addition, a lecture is presented at the Annual General Meeting and at the Social Evening held during the National Honey Show. The subscription is £10.00 per annum, £12.00 for dual membership (one copy only of publications).

COUNTY BEEKEEPING MAGAZINES AND NEWSLETTERS

AVON, Ms Julie Young
1 Church Cottages
Abson Road, Abson Wick
Bristol, BS30 5TT
0117 937 2156
julieyoung@btinternet.
com
BEDFORDSHIRE, Sue Lang
154a Lower Shelton
Road, Upper Shelton
Marston Moretaine
Beds, MK43 0LS
01234 764180
07879 848550
bedfordshirehoney@
hotmail.co.uk
BERKSHIRE, Ron Crocker
25 Ship Lake Bottom
Peppard Common
Oxon RG9 5HH
CAMBRIDGESHIRE,
Mr. Chris Evans
7 The Furlongs,
Needingworth,
St. Ives,
Cambs. PE27 4TX
CHESHIRE,Pete Sutcliffe
2 Hatfield Court
Holmes Chapel,
Cheshire, CW4 7HP
h.p.sutcliffe@googlemail.
com.

CHESTERFIELD & DISTRICT
Mrs Margaret Edge
4 Cinder Hill,
Shireoaks,
Worksop, S81 8NR
CORNWALL, Gillian Searle
6 Harleigh Road, Bodmin
Cornwall PL31 1AQ
CUMBRIA, Dave Bates
Greenfield House
Low Green
Temple Sowerby
Penrith CA10 1SD
DERBYSHIRE, Mrs. M. Cowley
14 Montpelier, Quorndon
Derby DE22 5JW
DEVON, Glyn R Davies
Landscore
Eastern Rd,Ashburton
Devon TQ13 7AR
01364 652640
landscore@eclipse.co.uk
DORSET, Richard Norman
19, Broughton Crescent
Wyke Regis, Weymouth
Dorset, DT4 9AS
DURHAM, Ian Copinger
9 Green Court, Esh,
Durham DH1 9RY
0191 3730249
copinger@tiscali.co.uk

ESSEX, Pat Allen
8 Franks Cottages
St Mary's Lane
Upminster RM14 3NU
GLOUCESTERSHIRE, Mrs A Ellis
19 Whaddon Road
Cheltenham
Gloucestershire GL52 5LZ
GUERNSEY BKA
Ruth Collins
Colombier House
Torteval
Guernsey GY8 0NF
GWENT, Bridget Woodhead
Stonewall Cottage
Warrage Road, Raglan
Gwent NP15 2LD
HAMPSHIRE, John Hanks
Mayville, East Dean Road
Lockerley
Romsey SO51 0JQ
tel/fax 01794 340541
johnhanks@btinternet.com
HEREFORDSHIRE, Mr. L.en Dixon
The Square,
Titley Kington, HR5 3RG
beeline2ljd@yahoo.co.uk

BEE MAGS

✉ ☎

HERTFORDSHIRE
Paul Cooper
01279 771231
HUNTINGDON
Wilma Vaughan
Lauriston Copse
Warboys, Huntingdon
Cambs PE28 2US
KENDAL & SOUTH
WESTMORLAND
Roger Blocksidge
20 Fowl Ing Lane
Kendal
Cumbria
LA9 6HB
tinky_winky@
hotmail.com
KENT,John Hendrie
26, Coldharbour
Lane,Hildenborough,
Tonbridge Kent
TN11 9JT
LEEDS BEEKEEPER
Editor Bill Cadmore,
104 Hall Lane
Horsforth, Leeds
LS18 5JG
0113 2160482
leeds.
bill.cadmore@
ntlworld.com
LEICS. & RUTLAND
Editor, T. Strachan
54 Burgess Rd.
Coalville,
Leicestershire LE67 3PX
terry@trs-net.co.uk

LINCOLNSHIRE, P. Raines
Grange Cottage
21 Humberston Av.
Humberstone
Grimsby DN36 4SL
LONDON, Steve Bembow
156 D evon Mansions
Tooley Street
London SE1 2NR
MEDWAY, Rob Smith
robert_787@hotmail.
com
Or: robert.m.smith@csl.
gov.uk
MOLE A. CLUB,
Dennis Cutler
70 Hurst Road
East Molesey
Surrey KT8 9AG
NEWCASTLE, George Batey
Rift Farm Cottage
Wylam NE41 8BL
NORFOLK, Michael Lancefield
Candlemas House
Fakenham Road
Stanhoe
King's Lynn PE31 8PX
lancefield@aol.com
NOTHAMPTONSHIRE
Roger G Virgo
5 Surfleet Close, Corby
Northamptonshire
NN18 9BG
amellifera@aol.com
NOTTINGHAMSH,
Stuart Ching
122 Marshall Hill Drive
Porchester
Notts NG3 6HW

SOMERSET, Richard Bache
6 Badgers Cross
Somerton
TA11 7JB
07815 799 126
newsletter@somerset
beekeepers.org.uk
SUFFOLK, Tony Molesworth
Kizimbani, Bildeston
Road, Combs. IP14 2JZ
tony.molesworth@essex.
businesslink.co.uk
WARWICKSHIRE, Rob Jones
124 Ashfurlong Road
Sutton Coldfield
B75 6EW
0121 378 0562
wbeditor@warwickshire-
beekeepers.org.uk
WILTSHIRE,
Ronald A Hoskins,
10 Larksfield
Covingham Park
Swindon SN3 5AD
WORCESTER,
Mrs U Brandwood
10 Monnow Close
Droitwich
Worcester WR9 8T
Ursula@brandwoodu.
freeserve.co.uk
YORKSHIRE
Newsletter Editor,
Bill Cadmore,
104 Hall Lane, Horsforth
Leeds LS18 5JG
0113 216 0482
bill.cadmore@
ntlworld.com

CONBA UK, COUNCIL OF THE NATIONAL BEEKEEPING ASSOCIATIONS IN THE UNITED KINGDOM

CONBA was established in 1978 to promote the aims and objectives of the national beekeeping associations of England, Scotland, Ulster and Wales. Its purpose is to represent the interests of beekeepers' with local, national and international authorities. A representative delegate from each of the member country associations occupies the chair for a period of two years, on a rotational basis.

The council meets twice per year, normally at Stoneleigh and at the National Honey Show in London, with the remaining meeting by rotation in the member association's country. Council business consists of any matters of common interest to all its members.

CONBA provides representation of its membership at the European Union (EU) through two specific committees, COPA and COGECA (COPA – Comite des Organisations Professionelles Agricoles de la CEE); (COGECA Comite de la Cooperation Agricole de la CEE); and the Honey Working Party (HWP).

The Honey Working Party meetings are held at Brussels. This committee liases with the European Commission in relation to apicultural matters concerning the member states of the European Union (EU). These matters are subsequently presented to the European Parliament for its consideration, implementation or revision or rejection. The subsequent approval of such matters results in establishing legislation, government support and possible EC funding relating to the practice of apicultural production in the UK through its membership of the EU.

INCORPORATING THE BEEKEEPING ORGANISATIONS OF:
England, Channel Islands Isle of Man, Scotland, Ulster, Wales

SECRETARY
Michael J. Badger MBE MA
Kara, 14 Thorn Lane
Roundhay, Leeds, LS8 1NN
0113 2945 879
fax 0113 2250 550
E-mail, (week-days)
buzz.buzz@ntlworld.com
E-mail, (week-ends)
buzz.buzz@surfanytime.net

CHAIRMAN, Ian Craig
30 Burnside Avenue
Brookfield,Johnstone,
Renfrewshire , PA5 8UT
ian@iancraig.wanado.co.uk

VICE-CHAIRMAN, Dinah Sweet
Graigfawr Lodge,
Caerphilly CF83 1NF
sweetd@cardiff.ac.uk

HON. TREASURER, David Salkild
256 Gower Road, Sketty
Swansea, Wales SA2 9JL
01792 205 822
d.salkilld1936@btinternet.com

CONBA

138

DEVON APICULTURAL RESEARCH GROUP

DARG is an independent group of experienced enthusiastic beekeepers whose primary aim is to collect and analyse data on matters of topical interest which may assist their apicultural education and promote the advancement of beekeeping. At their monthly meetings, DARG members discuss various topics in open forum, during which they exchange ideas and information from their personal beekeeping knowledge and experience. They also undertake suitable research projects which further the Group's aims.

TOPICS CURRENTLY BEING UNDERTAKEN
• Use of Shook Colonies and Comb Change in the control of brood diseases.
• Methods of Integrated Pest Management for the control of varroa.
• Honeybee genetics with particular reference to the selection of breeder queens.
• A survey of Useful bee plants, shrubs and trees in the South West.

PUBLICATIONS AVAILABLE
• **The Beeway Code.** A common sense guide for beginners to help avoid problems with neighbours and produce a safe and peaceful apiary.
• **Seasonal Management.** A useful aid to planning your work effectively
• **Living with Varroa jacobsoni.** A best selling title and an invaluable weapon in winning the war against the mite - updated in 1999
• **Queen Rearing.** Providing detailed help in rearing new queens in order to promote vigorous colonies.
• **Selection of Apiary Sites** full of tips for choosing the right sites for your bees.

CHAIRMAN, Richard Ball
Stoneyford Farmhouse
Colaton Raleigh
Sidmouth
Devon EX10 0HZ
HON SECRETARY, Kingsley Law
Halwell Farm, Denbury
Newton Abbot, TQ12 6ED
0180 381 2285

PUBLICATIONS OFFICER, David Loo
25 Woodlands
Newton-St-Cyres, Exeter
Devon EX5 5BP
0139 285 1472

TREASURER, Bob Ogden
Pennymoor Cottage
Pennymoor
Tiverton
Deven EX16 8LJ
01363 866687

All titles cost £2.50 per copy (post free) from the Publications Officer (tel. 01392 851472). Discounts are available for BBKA affiliated Associations
Please contact the Publications Officer for details

EAS

✉ ☎

THE EASTERN APICULTURAL
SOCIETY OF NORTH AMERICA

www.easternapiculture.org

Kathy Summers, 623 West Liberty Street, Medina Ohio 44256
Kathy@BeeCulture.com

The Eastern Apicultural Society of North America www.easternapiculture.org) holds its annual Short Course and Conference the first full week of August, 2009, at Holiday Valley Resort and Conference Center, in Ellicotville, New York. Ellicotville is in western New York, just south of Buffalo, New York. Holiday Valley is a superb setting for this conference with first rate facilities.

We start with our intensive 3-day, 2-level Short Course, …a starter's course, taught by our own EAS Master Beekeepers, focusing on on keeping your bees healthy and alive; and an advanced course looking at a variety of topics for experienced beekeepers. A new feature will be our anatomy class…look for that extra in the program one evening. There is plenty of hands-on bee work at our Conference, with 20 on-site colonies available, and a commercial queen breeding yard just down the road.

The theme for this year's Conference is "Toward Chemical Free Beekeeping". Speakers include Dr. Tom Rinderer from the USDA Honey Bee Research Lab at Baton Rouge, Louisiana, who developed the Russian Honey Bee, and Bob Brachman, commercial Russian Queen Breeder, Kirk Webster Kent Williams and Mike Palmer will also be there. They successfully use Russians in their operatons.

Other speakers include Dr. Tom Seeley and Dr. Nick Calderone from Cornell, Dr. Dave Tarpy from North Carolina, Dr. Jeff Pettis, USDA Research Leader and the best source of information on Colony Collapse Disorder and more.

Plus, there's Commercial beekeeper Andy Card and his family's operation right there in Ellicotville who run just over 20,000 colonies in New England and Louisiana, moving half to California to pollinate almonds. One of Andy's largest extraction facilities is here and tours show how he manages his operation to make honey and pollinate crops. And don't forget our many Vendors who have everything new in beekeeping available onsite.

Watch our web page at www.easternapiculture.org for updates and secure online registration beginning in May or so. For more information contact Kim Flottum at Kim@BeeCulture.com.

THE FEDERATION OF IRISH BEEKEEPERS' ASSOCIATIONS

http://www.irishbeekeeping.ie

Comhnascadh Cumann Beachairi na hEireann

ANNUAL SUMMER COURSE

The 2010 Beekeeping Summer Course held at the Franciscan College, Gormanston, Co Meath will take place from 26th of July to Saturday 31st July 2010. Guest Speaker will be Mr Dewey Caron from the University of Delaware, America. Dewey is Professor of Entomology & Applied Ecology at the College of Agricultural & National Resources at the University of Delaware, USA.

Full course including accommodation and meals €310. For reservation, send deposit of €40 to Summer Course Convenor: Mr Gerry Ryan, Deerpark, Dundrum, Co Tipperary (062-71274) or Email ryansfancy@gmail.com

PUBLICATIONS

• **Beekeeping in Ireland - A History** - J.K. Watson
This book gives the history of the craft from time immemorial to the present. It is well bound, hard backed and excellently presented. There are 293 pages of valuable information and 53 pictures of prominent beekeepers past and present. Price €7.00

• **Bees, Hives and Honey** - Published by F.I.B.K.A. - Edited by Eddie O'Sullivan.
This book has been compiled from writings by some of Ireland's most prominent beekeepers of the present day. It is an instruction book on beekeeping published as a millennium project and should prove a modern treatise on the craft of beekeeping and its associated products. There are over 200 pages, also many photographs and illustrations. Price €12.70 (Paperback) or €19 (Hardback)
Available from Eddie O'Sullivan, Phone: 021-4542614, Email : eosbee@indigo.ie

HON. SECRETARY
Mr. Michael G. Gleeson
Ballinakill Enfield Co. Meath
046 9541433
e-mail, mgglee@eircom.net

PRESIDENT
Mr Dennis Ryan
Mylerstown, Clonmel, Co Tipperary, 052 25600
Email dryan266@eircom.net

VICE PRESIDENT
Mr Seamus Reddy
8 Tower View Park, Kildare, 045 521945
Email
seamusreddy@eircom.net

PRO Mr P.McCabe,
"Sherdara"
Beuaulieu Cross
Drogheda, Co. Louth
041 983 6159
philipmccabe@eircom.net
HON. EDITOR, Jim Ryan
Innisfail, Kickham Street
Thurles, Co Tipperary
0504 22228
jimbee1@eircom.net

FIBKA

✉ ☎

HON. MANAGER, Mr. David Lee
Scart, Kildorry, Co. Cork
022 25595
davidleej@eircom.net

HON. TREASURER,
Mrs Bridie Terry
"Ait na Greine", Coolbay
Cloyne, Midleton,Co Cork
0214652141
aitnagreine@gmail.com

EDUCATION OFFICER
Dr. Brendan Coughlan
Ard na gCloch, Corcullen
Moycullen, Co. Galway
091 555211
B.OCochlain@irishbroad-band.net

LIBRARIAN Jim Ryan.
Innisfail, Kickham Sr
Thurles,co Tipperary
jimbee1@eircom.net

SUMMER COURSE CONVENER
Mr Gerry Ryan
Deerpark, Dundrum,
Co Tipperary
062 71274
ryansfancy@gmail.com

HONEY SHOW SECRETARY
Mr R Williams
Tincurry
Cahir
Co Tipperary
052 7442617
emwilliams@eircom.net

- **The Irish Bee Guide** - Reverend J.D. Dgges
First published in 1904, It was proclaimed as an excellent book on beekeeping. It also won a place as a notable production in the literary context. It eventually ran to sixteen editions and sold seventy-six thousand copies overall. The name was changed in the second issue to The Practical Bee Guide. Now, one hundred years later, a decision has been taken to honour this great work. What better way to do it than to re-issue the book as it was in 1904 when it first entered the literary world. The re-print is an exact replica of the original first edition. The price per copy is Hardback €30 and Softback €20
Available from Eddie O'Sullivan, Phone : 021-4542614,
Email: eosbee@indigo.ie

- **An Beachaire** - The Irish Beekeeper
the monthly organ of FIBKA, subscription £20.00 Stg post free from The Manager. Readership of the Journal in Northern Ireland carries third party insurance public liability cover up to €6.500,000 on any one claim and product liability cover up to €6.500,000 on any one claim, on payment of £5.00 Stg extra.

LIBRARY
The library is owned and controlled by FIBKA. It contains very many valuable books ancient and modern, available to members for return postage only. The Librarian is Jim Ryan, Innisfail, Kickham Street, Thurles, Co Tipperary.
Email: jimbee1@eircom.net

CORRESPONDENCE COURSES
The Examination Board has sponsored correspondence courses for candidates preparing for the Intermediate and Senior (Bee Masters) Examinations. Applications to John Cunningham, Ballygarron, Kilmeaden, Co Waterford, Tel No 051-399897/086-8399108 Email: john3cunningham@hotmail.com

EXAMINATIONS
The Board conducts five grades of examinations at the annual Summer Course at Gormanston College: Preliminary, Intermediate, Senior, Lecturer and Honey Judge. Preliminary and Intermediate Examinations are also held at Provincial centres in May each year.

EDUCATION
The Federation Examinations are recognised as Third Level Examinations by the National Council for Educational Awards (NCEA), thus candidates who pass the Senior Examination may apply to the NCEA for a National Certificate in Science (Apiculture) and candidates who have passed the Lectureship

Examination and who have at least two years' experience as Lecturers and who have also gained a sufficient standing in the beekeeping community may apply to the NCEA for a Diploma in Science (Apiculture), these awards are conferred by the Cork Institute of Technology (CIT) under a programme of Experiential Learning, for the Diploma a comprehensive Portfolio must be submitted to CIT, successful candidates are entitled to use the qualification NatDipSc (Apic).

Courses for beginners are run by Affiliated Associations and the FIBKA holds an Annual Summer Course in Gormanston College in July. The course caters for the three grades of students: beginners, intermediate, and senior and covers the theory and practice of modern apiculture. Examinations are held in these grades and also at Honey Judge and Lecturer level. Further information on the Examinations may be obtained from the Education Officer, Dr Brendan Coughlan, Chemistry Department, National University of Ireland, Galway (e-mail : B.OCochlain@irishbroadband.net)

NATIONAL HONEY SHOW

This is held at Gormanston College in conjunction with the annual Beekeeping Course. The Schedule contains 32 Open Classes and 3 Confined classes with €1,000 in prizes. Over 30 Challenge Cups and Trophies are presented for the competition.

Honey Show Secretary: Mr Redmond Williams, Tincurry, Cahir, Co Tipperary Tel No 052-7442617 e-mail: emwilliams@eircom.net

INSURANCE

The limit of indemnity of public liability policy is €6.500,000 arising from one accident or series of accidents. There is also product liability of €6.500,000 arising from any one claim. The policy extends to all registered affiliated members whose subscriptions are fully paid up on the 31st December of any one year and whose names are entered in the FIBKA register held by the Treasurer.

LIFE VICE PRESIDENTS

Mr. M.I Moynihan
41 Caseyville, Dungarvan
Co. Waterford
058 42389

Mr. P. O'Reilly
11 Our Lady's Place,
Naas Co. Kildare
045 897568

Mr. M.L. Woulfe
Railway House, Midleton
Co. Cork
021 631011

Mrs Frances Kane
Firmount, Clane,
Co Kildare,
087 2450640
or 045 893150

ASSOCIATION SECRETARIES

ASHFORD, Mr Michael Giles
55 Saunders Lane, Rathnew,
Co Wicklow
086-8369152

BANNER,Ms Aoife Nic Giolla
Blossom Lodge, Derra,
Kilkisken, Co Clare.
087 6743030

CARBERY, MrSean O'Donovan
Drominidy, Drimologue
Co Cork, 087 7715001

CARLOW, Mr. John Lennon
31 Idrone Park, Tullow Road,
Carlow   059 9141315

CO. CAVAN, Ms Christine Grey
Tullyvin, Cootehill, Co Craven
049 5553164

CO. CORK, Mr Robert McCutcheon
Clancoolemore, Bandon,
Cork. 023-41714

CO. DONEGALMr Derek Byrne
Carrick West, Laghey
Co.Donegal
074 9722340

CO. DUBLIN, Mr Liam McGarry
24 Quinns Road, Shankill,
Co Dublin.
087-2643492

CO. GALWAY,
Dr. Brendan Coughlan
Ard na gCloch, Corcullen,
Galway
091 555211

CO. KERRY, Mr Ruary Rudd
Westgate, Waterville,
Co. Kerry
066 9474251

CO. LIMERICK, Mr. Sean Flavin
Creeves Cross,
Shanagolden, Co. Limerick
069 60328

FIBKA

✉ ☎

CO. LOUTH,
Ms Patricia Finlay Hanratty
Grey Acre, Kilkerley,
Dundalk, Co Louth.
042-9329153 or 087-0640413

CO. LONGFORD,
Mrs Brigit Koston
Sunnyside House
Loughgowna, Co. Cavan
043 83285

CO. MAYO Mrs. Cathy Dunne,
Cloofinish, Swinford,
Co. Mayo 094 9252543

CO. OFFALY,
Mr Cyril Page
Woodford, Loughrea,
Co Galway.
0906-749025/086-8043072

CO. WATERFORD
Mr Pat Dillane,
Coolbagh, Clashmore,
Co. Waterford
02496979

CO. WEXFORD
Mr. Padraig McKenna
Blake Cottage, Curracloe,
Co. Wexford

DUNHALLOW,
Mr Andrew Bourke,
Pallas, Lombardstown,
Mallow, Co Cork
087 2783807

DUNAMAISE,
Mr Seamus Brennan
Bondra,Colt,
Ballyroan, Co Laois
057 8731871

DUNMANWAY,
Mr. Michael l O'Sullivan
Ballyhalwick Dunmanway,
Co. Cork (023) 45257

EAST CORK, Mr C Terry
"Ait na Graine", Coolbay
Cloyne, Co. Cork
021 4652141

EAST WATERFORD
Mr. Michael Hughes
51 Woodlawn Grove

Cork St, Waterford
051 373461

FINGAL, Mr John McMullan
34 Ard na Mara Crescent
Malahide, Co. Dublin
(01) 8450193

FOYLE, P J Costello
Lr Drumaiveir, Greencastle
Co Donegal
074 9381303

GOREY, Mr Joe Nealon
Aspen Woods,
Raheenteigue, Tinahely,
Co Wicklow.
0402-38481

INNISHOWEN,
Mr Paddy McDonagh,
Milltownwn, Carndonagh
Co. Donegal 074 9374881

KILLORGLIN, Mr Mike Cronin
Upper Tullig,
Killorglin, Co Kerry
066-9769892

KILTERNAN
Ms. Mary Montaut
4 Mount Pleasant Villas
Bray, Co. Wicklow
01 2860497

MID KILKENNY,
Mr John Ryan
Kiltown, Castlecomer,
Co Kilkenny.
056-4441375

NEW ROSS,
Mr Seamus Kennedy
Churchtown, Fethard-on-Sea,
New Ross, Co. Wexford
051 397259

NORTH CORK, Mr Moss Guiry
Belview, Bruree, Co Limerick
061-397040

NORTH KILDARE, Mr Sean Byrne
53 Moorfielf Park,
Newbridge, Co. Kildare
045 432048

NORTH MONAHGAN
Mrs Joanna McGlaughlin
35 CastleLane,
Caledon,
Co. Tyrone, BT68 4UB
048 37569548

NORTH TIPPERARY,
Mr. Jim Ryan
"Innisfail" Kirkham St
Thurles, Co. Tipperary
0504 22228

ROUNDWOOD, Mrs M O'Byrne
Carrig View, Moneystown
South, Roundwood,
Wicklow 0404 45209

S. KILDARE,
Mr Mike Cummins
Garretfield, Donard,
Co Wicklow.
087-2726177

S. KILKENNY,
Mr Richard Moran
Kilbline, Bennetsbridge,
Co Kilkenny.
056-7727457

S. TIPPERARY, Mr Tom Prendergast
Ballypatrick, Clonmel,
Co Tipperary
087 9109360

S. WEST CORK,Mr John Bryan
Currarane,Kilbrittan,
Co Cork, 023 49625

S. WEXFORD,Mr James Hogan
Castlebridge,
Co Wexford,
053 9159202

SUCK VALLEY, Mr Frank Kenny
Stonepark, Roscommon
0906 626156

THE KINGDOM, Mr Jim Clerkin,
Arabella House
Ballymacelligott,Tralee
Co Kerry,
066 7137611

THE MIDLAND BEEKEEPERS
Mr Jim Donohoe
11 New Ballinderry, Mullingar,
Co Westmeath
044-9340771/086-2555729

THE ROYAL CO
Mrs Martina Keegan
Grange, Bective, Navan,
Co Meath, 046 9029216

WEST CORK
Mr Donald Hanley
Bawnard, Eyeries,
Co Cork,
027 74187

144

INTERNATIONAL BEE RESEARCH

ASSOCIATION WEB http://www.ibra.org.uk

I B R A

INTERNATIONAL
BEE RESEARCH
ASSOCIATION

IBRA — the International Bee Research Association — Aiming to inspire, promote and publicize research in apiculture and the value of bees. A charity devoted to advancing apicultural education and science worldwide. Since its formation in 1949 IBRA has worked to serve the information needs of beekeepers, scientists, advisers, teachers and many other groups. Technically-minded beekeepers in the UK and in other countries find IBRA's journals and library services uniquely valuable.

CORRESPONDENCE TO:
DIRECTOR, Richard Jones
International Bee Research Association
16 North Road
Cardiff CF10 3DY
029 2037 2409
Fax: 05601 135640
E-mail, mail@ibra.org.uk

PUBLICATIONS
Journal of Apicultural Research incorporating Bee World, publishing bee science that's worldwide and world class, this award winning journal provides beekeepers and scientists with the latest information and research.
Journal of ApiProduct and ApiMedical Science, is a new electronic journal dedicated to publishing the latest research on the therapeutic properties of hive products. Both these journals provide highest quality, peer reviewed information.
Buzz Extra, the world view on bees and beekeeping! This topical and informative publication grows in content and popularity, and covers everything from bee history to the latest up dates on colony collapse.

WORLD WIDE WEB
IBRA also provides a free information service on the World Wide Web. Visit our pages at:
http://www.ibra.org.uk

145

IBRA

✉ ☎

LIBRARY

For the first time, a full catalogue of what is in the Eva Crane /IBRA library will be available on our web site. Accessing information will then be just a click away via links to the national library of Wales that will house the collection in a modern cotrolled environment. Information will continue to be available on request from the Nation Library with accessibility maintained and aided by professional librarians.

PUBLICATION SALES

The bookshop is accessible via the web site selling IBRA publications and a small range of other publications relevant to bees and international beekeeping activities. This activity is ti publicise and support our own work.

MEMBERSHIP

The key to IBRA's work is the support it receives from members. Their subscriptions (40.00 per year) form the overwhelming part of IBRA's income. Members receive for their subscription the quarterly journal and a reduction on purchases from the IBRA shop. They are welcome to contribute, encouraged to be active in their support and can be sure that they are making a real contribution to the collection, collation and dissemination of bee information on an international scale.

APIS-UK
WWW.beedata.COM

The FREE monthly beekeeping magazine
bringing you NEWS, REVIEWS & TOPICAL TIPS
for all beekeepers directly to your computer

REGISTER TODAY @
beedata.com

THE INSTITUTE OF NORTHERN IRELAND BEEKEEPERS (INIB)

www.inibeekeepers.com

Annual Conference 7th November 2009.
Hosted by Roe Valley beekeepers Association
Annual Honey Show 21st November 2009.

Objects of the Institute

The Institute is established to advance the service of apiculture and to promote and foster the education of the people of Northern Ireland and surrounding environs without distinction of age, gender, disability, sexual orientation, nationality, ethnic identity, political or religious opinion, by associating the statutory authorities, community and voluntary organisations and the inhabitants in a common effort to advance education, and in particular:

a) to raise awareness amongst the beneficiaries about bees, bee-keeping and methods of management;

b) to foster an atmosphere of mutual support among bee-keepers and to encourage the sharing of information and provision of helpful assistance amongst each other.

Affiliation

INIB is affiliated to the British Beekeepers Association.

With 14,000 members the British Beekeepers Association (BBKA) is the leading organisation representing beekeepers within the UK.

As an INIB member, affiliation gives the following benefits.

- BBKA News
- Public Liability Insurance
- Product Liability Insurance
- Bee Disease Insurance available
- Free Information Leaflets to Download
- Members Password Protected Area and Discussion Forum
- Correspondence Courses
- Examination and Assessment Programme
- Telephone Information
- Research Support
- Legal advice
- Representation and lobbying of Government, EU and official bodies.

Clogher Valley Beekeepers Association is affiliated to INIB
Email: cloghervalley@onlineni.net

IBRA ✉ ☎

Events
The Institute holds an annual conference and honey show.
The institute brings to Northern Ireland world renowned expert
speakers from USA and Europe to give talks to beekeepers on
the latest research and up to date beekeeping methods.

Education
Demonstrations on various topics such as mead making,
preparing honey for shows are held during the year.
Courses for honey judges are available.

Honey Bees On Line Studies
As a result of our Association with Professor Jurgen Tautz of
BEEgroup Biozentrum Universitaet Wuerzburg INIB is delighted
to have introduced Honey Bees On Line Studies into Wallace
High School, Lisburn a unique world wide project for schools to
study bees on line. http://www.beegroup.de

SECRETARY
Caroline Thomson
105 Cidercourt Road
Crumlin
BT29 4RX
02894453655
bridgeconsultancy@
ni-home.co.uk

CHAIRMAN
Michael Young MBE
101 Carnreagh,
Hillsborough
BT26 6LJ
 02892689724
myoungjudge@
yahoo.co.uk

Holders of the Institute of Northern Ireland Beekeepers Honey Judge Certificate

001. MICHAEL BADGER MBE	01132 945879	BUZZ.BUZZ@NTLWORLD.COM
002. GAIL ORR	02892 638363	GAIL.ORR@BELFASTTRUST.HSCNI.NET
003. CECIL MCMULLAN	02892 638675	MADELINE.MCMULLAN@HOTMAIL.CO.UK
004. HUGH MCBRIDE	02825 640872	LORRAINE.MCBRIDE@CARE4FREE.NET
005. LORRAINE MC BRIDE	02825 640872	LORRAINE.MCBRIDE@CARE4FREE.NET
006. BILLY DOUGLAS	02897 562926	
007. MICHAEL YOUNG MBE	02892 689724	MYOUNGJUDGE@YAHOO.CO.UK
008. FRANCIS CAPENER	01303 254579	FRANCIS@HONEYSHOW.FREESERVE.CO.UK
009. MARGARET DAVIES	01202 526077	MARG@JDAVIES.FREESERVE.CO.UK
010. IAN CRAIG	01505 322684	IAN'AT'IANCRAIG.WANADOO.CO.UK
011. DINAH SWEET	02920 756483	
012. HENRY J FERGUSON	01550 777132	
013. LESLIE M WEBSTER	01466 771351	LESWEBSTER@MICROGRAM.CO.UK
014. REDMOND WILLIAMS	003535242617	EMWILLIAMS@EIRCOM.NET
015. TERRY ASHLEY	01270 760757	TERRY.ASHLEY@FERA.GSI.GOV.UK
016. IVOR FLATMAN	01924 257089	IVORFLATMAN@SUPANET.COM
017. ALAN WOODWARD	01302 868169	JANET.WOODWARD@VIRGIN.NET
018. DENNIS ATKINSON	01995 602058	DHMATKINSON@TESCO.NET
019 LEO MCGUINNESS	028711811043	PMCGUINNESS@GLENDERMOTT.COM
020 TOM CANNING	02838871260	TOM.CANNING@VIRGIN.NET

USA
019. ROBERT BREWER		RBREWER@ARCHES.UGA.EDU
020. ANN HARMAN		AHWORKERB@AOL.COM
021. BOB COLE		

LASI

⊠ ☎

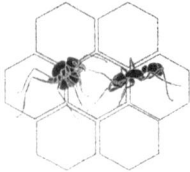

LABRATORY OF APICULTURE & SOCIAL INSECTS (LASI)

UNIVERSITY OF SUSSEX

FURTHER INFORMATION CONTACT
PDr. Francis L. W. Ratnieks,
Professor of Apiculture
Laboratory of Apiculture &
Social Insects (LASI)
Department of Biological &
Environmental Science
University of Sussex, Falmer,
Brighton BN1 9QG, UK

tel: 01273 872954 (landline),
07766270434 (mob)
F.Ratnieks@Sussex.ac.uk

LASI was founded in 1995 and is headed by Dr. Francis Ratnieks, who is the UK's only Professor of Apiculture. Professor Ratnieks received his training in honey bee biology in the USA at Cornell University and at the University of California. Also in the USA, he was a part-time commercial beekeeper with up to 180 hives used for almond pollination and comb honey production.

From 1995 to 2007 LASI was based at the University of Sheffield. In February 2008 Professor Ratnieks moved to the University of Sussex. Sussex University has provided a new laboratory that is ideal for honey bee research. There is a large adjoining apiary with an equipment shed and workshop, and the laboratory is only 100m from the main biology building. There are further apiaries on the university campus just 5 minutes walk away.

LASI is the largest university-based laboratory studying honey bees in the UK and is set up both to do research on honey bee biology and to train the next generation of honey bee scientists. Undergraduate students can do research projects on honey bee biology in their final year, and also receive lectures on honey bee biology. Graduate students can take a PhD in a particular area of honey bee biology. Postdoctoral researchers study honey bees and learn new skills to complement the training they received while doing their PhD.

LASI research focuses on both basic and applied questions in honey bee biology and beekeeping. Research areas include: how honey bees organize their colonies, how they resolve their conflicts, nestmate recognition and guarding, foraging, mating, improved beekeeping techniques, bee health and breeding, conservation of native honey bees.

LASI's mission is to be an international centre of research excellence, to train the next generation of bee researchers, and to be a resource for UK beekeepers and the public in general.

(INTER/) NATIONAL PERIODICALS

AMERICAN BEE JOURNAL
(US monthly)
Agents: E.H. Thorne (Beehives) Ltd
Wragby, Lincoln
AUSTRALASIAN BEEKEEPER
AUSTRALIAN BEE JOURNAL
(Monthly. Subscriptions
US$38
Sample from: Penders PMB
19 Maitland, NSW 2320
Australia
BEE CRAFT
Official monthly journal
of the British Beekeepers
Association
Subscriptions and enquiries to:
Sue Jakeman
Bee Craft Ltd
107 Church St,
Werrington
Peterborough
PE4 6QF
secretary@bee-craft.com
www.bee-craft.com
01733 771221
BEEKEEPERS QUARTERLY, THE
Companion to the
Beekeepers Annual
Subscriptions £25 p.a (but
group schemes at reduced
rates exist for BKAs)

from: Northern Bee Books
Scout Bottom Farm
Mytholmroyd, Hebden
Bridge, W. Yorkshire HX7 5JS
**BERKSHIRE BEEKEEPERS
ASSOCIATIONS, FEDERATION OF
(FBBKA)**
Newsletter Editor,
Mr R F Crocker
25 Shiplake Bottom
Peppard Common
Oxon RG9 5HH
0118 9722315
berksbees@btopenworld.
com
CHESHIRE BEEKEEPER
The Newsletter of CBKA
Mr P Sutcliffe
2 Hatfield Court,
Holmes Chapel
Cheshire CW4 7HP
h.p.sutcliffe@googlemail.
com
GLEANINGS IN BEE CULTURE
US monthly
From: Northern Bee Books
Scout Bottom Farm,
Mytholmroyd, HX7 5JS
& E.H. Thorne Ltd
Beehive Works Wragby
LN3 5LA

**INDIAN BEE JOURNAL IN
ENGLISH**
1325 Sadashiv Peth, Poona
411 8030, India
**INTERNATIONAL BEE RESEARCH
ASSOCIATION**
free samples from
16 North Road
Cardiff
CF10 3DY
mail@ibra.org.uk
IRISH BEEKEEPER
(Monthly) Editor: Jim Ryan
Inisfail, Kickham Street
Thurles, Co. Tipperary
jimbee1@eircom.net
**THE NEW ZEALAND
BEEKEEPER JOURNAL**
Published 11 issues per year
for National BKA of
New Zealand
Contact: Pam Edwards
Executive Secretary
National Beekeepers
Association
10 Nikau Lane
R D 3
Otaki 5583
New Zealand
Tel: 64-6-362 6301
Fax: 64 6 362 6302
secretary@nba.org.nz

NAT MAGS

✉ ☎

BEEKEEPER, THE Magazine of the Scottish BKA. Membership terms **from:** Enid Brown, Milton House, Main Street, Scotlandwell Kinross-shire KY13 9JA Sample copy to view online www.scottishbeekeepers. org.uk

SOUTH AFRICAN BEE JOURNAL Bi-monthly. P.O. Box 41 Modderfontein, 1645, RSA.

THE SPEEDY BEE Monthly US newspaper, £24 **from:** NBB, Scout Bottom Farm, Mytholmroyd Hebden Bridge HX7 5JS

GWENYNWYR CYMRU / WELSH BEEKEEPER, EDITOR, Duncan Parks Cefn Coed Graianrmon yn lal Mold CH7 4QW 01824 780504 fax 01824 780822 e-mail, Duncan@The-Parks.com The publication of the Welsh Beekeepers Association giving news and views of beekeeping in Wales and abroad.

Golygydd/Editor: A Duncan Parks, Cefn Coed, Ffordd Graianrhyd, Llanarmon yn lal YR WYDDGRUG CH7 4QW (01824) 780 504 e-mail, duncan@the-parks.com **Erthyglau Cymraeg:** Dewi Morris Jones, Llwynderw Bronant Aberystwyth SY23 4TG Manylion tanysgrifau/ **Subscription Details:** H. I. Morris, Golygfan Llangynin, Sancler CAERFYRDDIN SA33 4JZ 01944 290885

THE NATIONAL DIPLOMA IN BEEKEEPING

The Examinations Board for the National Diploma in Beekeeping was set up in 1954 to meet a need for a beekeeping qualification above the level of the highest certificate awarded by the British, Scottish, Welsh and Ulster Associations.

The Diploma Examination, as designed by the Board, was considered to be an appropriate qualification for a County Beekeeping Lecturer or a specialist appointment requiring a high level of academic and practical ability in beekeeping. It is the highest beekeeping qualification recognised in the British Isles and a high percentage of the past and present holders of the Diploma have given distinguished service to beekeeping education at all levels.

Although the post of County Beekeeping Lecturer has now disappeared, this has merely emphasised the need for some beekeepers to face the challenge of this examination and maintain the high level skills and knowledge needed to keep pace with the increased problems facing all beekeepers at the present time.

The Board consists of representatives from a wide range of organisations and from Government Departments and together form an impressive amalgam of expert knowledge in Beekeeping and Education. Although the National Beekeeping Associations are represented on the Board it is entirely independent of them.

Normally the highest certificate of one of the National Associations is a necessary criterion for eligibility to take the Examination for the Diploma which is held in alternate years. The Written Examination is taken in March, and the Practical, in three sections plus a viva-voce is held in June.

The Board also organises an annual Advanced Beekeeping Course covering various parts of the syllabus that are difficult to cover by independent study. Lasting

HON. SECRETARY
Norman Carreck NDB
New Hall, Small Dole,
Henfield, West Sussex.
BN5 9YJ
01273 492206
norman.carreck@
btinternet.com

CHAIRMAN, Dr David Aston NDB
38 Wressle, Selby
YO8 6ET
01757 638758

a working week, they cover the main sections of the Syllabus and represent the highest level of training available to British Beekeepers at the present time. The outside lecturers are each acknowledged experts in their particular field. In recent years the Board have been privileged to hold their course at the CSL National Bee Unit at Sand Hutton, York.

For further details regarding the Diploma write, enclosing a stamped A4 SAE to the Secretary, or visit our website: http://www.national-diploma-bees.org.uk/

Those who have gained the National Diploma in Beekeeping

Matthew Allan	Celia Davis	Geoff Ingold	Fred Richards
Harry Allen	Ivor Davis	George Jenner	E. Roberts
Harrison Ashforth	Alec S.C. Deans	C. F. Jesson	Arthur Rolt
John Ashton	Clive de Bruyn	A.C. Kessel	Jeff Rounce
Dianne Askquith-Ellis	A.P. Draycott	W.E. Large	Graham Royle
David Aston	M. Feeley	G.W. Lumsden	J. Ryding
John Atkinson	Barry Fletcher	Henry Luxton	J.H. Savage
Miss E.E. Avey	David Frimston	A.S. McClymont	Donald Sims
Ken Basterfield	Oonagh Gabriel	J.L. MacGregor	F.G. Smith
Bridget Beattie	George Gill	Ian McLean	George Smith
Brig. H.T. Bell	Reg Gove	Ian A. Maxwell	J.H.F. Smith
R.W. Brooke	Eric Greenwood	Paul Metcalf	Robert Smith
Norman Carreck	Pam Gregory	J. Mills	Ken Stevens
Rosina Clark	Anthony R.W. Griffin	Bernhard Mobus	J. Swarbrick
Charles Collins	Robert Hammond	G. N'tonga	Margaret Thomas
Gerry Collins	Ben Harden	Peter Oldrieve	John Walker
Tom Collins	C.A. Harwood	Gillian Partridge	Adrian Waring
Robert Couston	Leslie Hender	E.H. Pee	Brian Welch
John Cowan	Alf Hebden	L.E. Perera	J. Wilbraham
S. J. Cox	Ted Hooper	E.R. Poole	
Jim Crundwell	Geoff Hopkinson	Bill Reynolds	
Beulah Cullen	G. Howatson	Pat Rich	

THE NATIONAL HONEY SHOW

www.honeyshow.co.uk
THE 2010 SHOW IS AT ST GEORGE'S COLLEGE,
WEYBRIDGE, SURREY KT15 2QS
28TH – 30TH OCTOBER.

This venue is excellent

Just off the M25 junction 11
Rail from Waterloo to Weybridge or Addlestone

Free car parking

The Show itself is a wonderful competitive exhibition
of all the products of the bee-hive, coupled with an
excellent series of lectures, workshops and a wide
variety of trade and educational stands.

We recommend that you attend all three days, and
suggest that you become a member of the Show –
just **£10.00** per annum

For further information, please write to the Hon General
Secretary, or Email: showsec@zbee.com or visit our
website www.honeyshow.co.uk

HON. GENERAL SECRETARY
REV. H.F CAPENER
1 Baldric Road
Folkestone CT20 2NR

HON TREASURER
C S Mence
27 Acacia Grove
New Malden, Surrey KT3 3BJ

PUT THIS DATE IN YOUR DIARY
28TH – 30TH OCTOBER 2010

RR

ROTHAMSTED RESEARCH

www.rothamsted.bbsrc.ac.uk

ROTHAMSTED RESEARCH
Plant and Invertebrate
Ecology Division
Harpenden
Hertfordshire AL5 2JQ
Tel (01582) 763133
Fax (01582) 760981

STAFF
Dr Juliet L Osborne
Dr. Judith Pell
Dr. Samantha Cook
Andrew P Martin
John Cussans
Jenny Swain
Jenny Jacobs
Penny Fletcher

Rothamsted is the oldest laboratory in the world devoted to agricultural research, having been established in 1843. Research on bees has been continuous since 1923 and current expertise is founded on pioneering work at Rothamsted by a number of eminent bee scientists. Approximately 20 honey bee colonies are now maintained for experimental purposes and the bee field station houses a behaviour laboratory, observation hive room and bee flight room as well as a workshop for the manufacture of specialised equipment.

The Rothamsted site provides a unique working environment with specialist modern equipment facilitating research on plant and microbial metabolites, molecular biology and synthetic and analytical chemistry. There is an experimental farm for complex field experiments, and there is a suite of glasshouses, controlled environment facilities, an insectary and a state of the art bioimaging suite housing three new electron microscopes and a confocal laser scanning microscope. Experimental design and analysis are backed up by excellent statistical, computing and library support.

BEE BEHAVIOUR AND POLLINATION ECOLOGY
We are investigating the interaction between bees, crops and the agricultural environment. The spatial and temporal foraging behaviour of honey bees and bumble bees within agricultural areas is being compared. Harmonic radar is being used to track flying bees, and other pollinators such as butterflies, to obtain new information about their flight paths, forage ranges, food preferences and orientation mechanisms. Bee-mediated pollen and gene

156

flow between plant populations is being investigated and quantified using genetic markers in white clover and oilseed rape.

A multidisciplinary approach to investigate bumble bee population dynamics is being taken, involving satellite imagery of the landscape together with field experiments and the use of genetic information. This will give a clearer picture of the status of bumblebee populations in the arable landscape and highlight land management practices that can help to reverse the decline in populations of these bees. This culminated in the National Bumblebee Nest Survey, 2004 (published in 2007): volunteers from all over the UK were asked to examine their gardens and the countryside to find bumblebee nests so that comparisons of habitat type can be made. The potential value of bee forage plants to enhance agricultural land for bees by providing a succession of pollen and nectar sources is also being investigated.

HONEY BEE PATHOLOGY
Rothamsted's research on the natural history and epidemiology of the infections and parasites of bees has had wide international recognition. However, research on honey bee pathology is currently suspended due to changes in funding available from Defra for bee health. Over the last 15 years, this work focused on Varroa destructor and the losses caused by honey bee virus infections that the mite transmits. In a collaborative project with Horticulture Research International (at University of Warwick), investigating potential biological control agents of V. destructor, the research identified and characterised fungal pathogens which are active against the mite but which are relatively safe for bees and other beneficial insects. Biological control offers an environmentally acceptable approach to the problem that could have considerable economic benefits, and we are actively seeking funding to continue this work.

INFORMATION EXCHANGE

Expertise in bee research is drawn upon by scientific colleagues world-wide and there are research links with institutes and universities in this country and abroad. Research findings are published in scientific journals but popular articles are also written for the beekeeping and agricultural press. Staff members serve on both national and international committees on diverse aspects of apiculture and a vigorous programme of lectures presented to national and local beekeeping associations ensures effective communication of recent work.

FUNDING

Rothamsted receives funds for research from the Biotechnology and Biological Sciences Research Council, through competitions and contracts from the Department for Environment, Food and Rural Affairs, the European Community, from Levy boards, commercial and other organisations. The support of the bee research programme in recent years by grants from the British Beekeepers Association and the C. B. Dennis British Beekeepers Research Trust is gratefully acknowledged.

For more information visit our web site: http://www.rothamsted.bbsrc.ac.uk

THE SCOTTISH BEEKEEPERS' ASSOCIATION

AIMS OF THE ASSOCIATION
- publish a monthly magazine
- maintain the Moir Library in Edinburgh
- conduct examinations in the art of beekeeping
- provide insurance and a compensation scheme for members

EDUCATION
The SBA arranges courses and awards certificates to successful candidates in the Scottish Basic Beemaster, Expert Beemaster, Honey Judge and Microscopy Examinations. It also actively promotes beekeeping by informing the public, especially the young, about bees and their benefits to the environment.

INSURANCE AND THE COMPENSATION SCHEME
All members of the SBA have insurance against Public Liability. The SBA Compensation Scheme is restricted to bee colonies located in Scotland and allocates part-replacement value for damage by vandalism, fire, theft and certain brood diseases.

LIBRARY
The SBA Moir Library in Edinburgh has one of the world's finest collection of beekeeping books. A library card is issued annually to every member who can borrow books at the cost of return postage only. Details may be obtained from the Library Convener.

MARKETS
Advice is given on all aspects of marketing honey products at appropriate times. Suggested bulk, wholesale and retail prices are notified in the magazine.

GENERAL SECRETARY
Mrs. Bronwen Wright
20 Lennox Road
Edinburgh EH5 3JW
(0131) 552 3439
e-mail, secretary@
scottishbeekeepers.org.uk

HON PRESIDENT
The Rt. Hon. Earl of Mansfield D.L, J.P
Scone Palace
Perth PH2 6BE

HON. VICE PRES,
Iain F Steven
4 Craigie View
Perth
PH2 0DP
01738 621100

HON. LIBRARIAN
Mrs. Margaret M. Sharp
City Librarian, City Library
George IV Bridge, Edinburgh

HON. LEGAL ADVISER,
Taggert, Meil & Mathers
20 Bon Accord Sq,
Aberdeen
(01224) 588020

SBA

✉ ☎

HON. AUDITOR, G. Hendry CA
20 Parkhill Crescent,
Dyce Aberdeen
(01224) 724247

PUBLICATIONS

• The Scottish Beekeeper is published monthly and sent post free as part of the annual membership fee of £25 payable to the Membership Convener.
• Introduction to Bees and Beekeeping is £2.00 plus postage and may be obtained from the Advertising and Publicity Convener.

PUBLICITY

Members can purchase the association tie, lapel badge, car sticker etc. Details may be obtained from the Advertising and Publicity Convener.

SHOWS

Three major annual honey shows are held in Scotland. They are at the Royal Highland Show, Ingliston, Edinburgh in June, while the Scottish National Honey Show and the East of Scotland Honey Show are both held at the Dundee Flower anf Food Festival in September. Shows are also held at Aberdeen, Ayr, Inverness and there are 2 shows in Fife.

Executive Committee

PRESIDENT, Alan Teale
8 Mayfield Road
Inverness IV2 4AE
01463 226411
teale@fs.com
VICE PRESIDENT,
Phil McAnespie
12 Monument Road
Ayr KA7 2RL
01292 885660
membership@
scottishbeekeepers.org.uk

IMM. PAST PRES,
Ian Craig
30 Burnside Avenue
Brookfield
Johnstone
Renfrewshire
PA5 8UT
01505 322684
ian@iancraig.
wanadoo.co.uk
GENERAL SEC
Mrs. Bronwen Wright
20 Lennox Road, Edinburgh
EH5 3JW (0131) 552 3439
secretary@
scottishbeekeepers.org.uk

SBA CO-ORDINATOR,
Iain F. Steven
4 Craigie View, Perth PH2 0DP
01738 621100
lomand@btinternet.com
TREASURER, Mrs. Barbara Cruden
Standing Stones, Dyce
Aberdeen AB21 0HH
(01224) 770001
EDITOR, SCOTTISH BEEKEEPER,
Nigel Hurst
11 Munro Way, Livingston,
West Lothian, EH54 8LP
01506 439384
editor@scottishbeekeepers.
org.uk

CONVENERS OF STANDING COMMITTEES

MEMBERSHIP CONVENER
P. McAnespie
12 Monument Rd.Ayr
KA7 2RL
01292 885660
membership@
scottishbeekeepers.org.uk
INSURANCE & COMPENSATION
C. Irwin
55 Lindsaybeg Rd
Chryston, Glasgow
G69 9DW
0141 7791333
ADVERTISING & PUBLICITY
Miss E Brown
Milton House, Main Street
Scotlandwell, Kinross
KY13 9JA
(01592) 840582
honeybees@onetel.com
EDUCATION, Ian Craig
30 Burnside Avenue
Brookfield. Johnstone
Renfrewshire PA5 8UT
01505 322684
ian@iancraig.wanadoo.
co.uk

SHOWS, Miss E Brown
Milton House, Main Street
Scotlandwell, Kinross
KY13 9JA
01592 840582
honeybees@onetel.com
LIBRARY, Mrs Una Robertson
13 Wardie Ave
Edinburgh
EH5 2AB
una.robertson@btinternet.
com
MARKETS, John Durkacz
15 Lundin Road
Crossford
Fife KY12 8PW
01383 722186
Durkacz@hotmail.co.uk
BEE DISEASES, Gavin Ramsay
8 Parkview
Station Road
Errol
Perth PH2 7SN
01821 642385
diseases@
scottishbeekeepers.org.uk

AREA REPRESENTATIVES
NORTH (ACTING),
Stella Forth
Kirkland Lodge
Wardlaw Road
Kirkhill
Inverness-shire IV5 7NB
01463 831511
gspceditor@live.co.u
EAST, Paul Gibson
7 Shielswood Court,
Galashiels, Selkirkshire
TD1 3RH
01896 750110
paulalisongibson@tiscali.
co.uk
WEST, Peter Stromberg
21 Woodside
Houston, Renfrewshire
PA6 7DD
01505 613830
pstromberg1@aol.com
ABERDEEN, Mrs. Hazel MacKenzie
Invercraig, Kingswell
Aberdeen . AB15 8PT
01224 740837
hazel@invercraig.
freeserve.co.uk

OFFICERS

AVA AND PROMOTION OF
BEEKEEPING,
W.B. Taylor
Newbigging Cottage
Drumlithie
Stonehaven AB39 3YA
(01569) 740375
e-mail,
williet.bee@virgin.net

WEBMASTER, Alisdair Joyce
Manachie Lodge.
Dallas Dhu
Forres
IV36 0RR
(01309) 671288
webmaster@
scottishbeekeepers.org.uk

SPRAY LIAISON,
Leslie N Webster
Birchlea
Rothiemay
Huntly
Aberdeenshire
AB54 7LN
(01466) 771351
leswebster@microgram.
co.uk

SBA

✉ ☎

S.B.A LECTURERS ★Addresses in SBA Honey Judges List
All those listed claim expenses (except G. Sharpe, Bees adviser funded by SGRD),
All speakers accompany talks with visual aids

★ **MISS. E. BROWN** (General)
01592 840542

★ **M BADGER** (General)
0113 2945879

★ **I. CRAIG** (General)
01505 322684

A.B. FERGUSON
(General, Varroa)
Firparkneuk. Kirtlebridge
Lockerbie   DG11 3LZ
01461 500322

★ **C. IRWIN** (General)
0141 7791333

★ **DR. F. ISLES** (Bee diseases)
01382 370 315

M.M. PETERSON
(Bee genetics)
Balhaldie House,
High street, Dunblane
FK15 0ER

01786 822093

MRS. U. A. ROBERTSON
(History of SBA, Moir Library,
History of beekeeping)
13 Wardie Ave
Edinburgh EH5 2AB
0131 552 5341

G. SHARPE (SAC) (Varroa
Management: My apiary
management system)
Apiculture Specialist
Life Science Technology
Group, SAC Auchincruive
Ayr KA6 5HW
01292 525375

★ **W.B. TAYLOR** (General)
01569 740375

★ **J. TYLER** (Strain selection
and queen breeding)
22 Montgomerie Drive

Fairlie, Ayrshire
01475 568421

★ **L. M. WEBSTER** (General)
01466 771351

DR G RAMSAY (Beekeeping
on the Internet / Can Bees
fight Varroa?)
Parkview, Station Road
Errol, Perth   PH2 7SN
01821 642385

A RIACH (Beehives through
the Ages)
Woodgate, 7 Newland Ave
Bathgate EH48 1EE
01506 653839

MEMBER ASSOCIATIONS AND THEIR SECRETARIES

ABERDEEN, Mrs Janice
Kennedy
13 Harvest Hill, Westhill
Aberdeen AB32 6PU
01224 743059

AYR, Mrs L Baillie
Windyhill Cottage
Uplands Rd, Sundrum
Ayre ,KA6 5JU
01292 570659

BORDER, A.F. Mitchell
30 Parkside, Coldstream
Berwickshire TD12 4DY
01890 882683

CADDONFOOT,
Mrs C Hamilton
Beechwood
Ormiston Terrace
Melrose
Roxburghshire
TD6 9SW
01896 820000
cathdech@gmail.com

CLYDE AREA, Mr George Morrison
102 Woodside Ave Bearsden
G61 2NZ
(0141) 942 9419

COWAL, Brian Madden
123a Alexandra Parade
Dunoon, PA23 8AW
01369 703317

DINGWALL
Mrs P. Piercy
Findon Mills,
Culbokie By Dingwall
Ross & Cromaty IV7 8JJ
01349 877401
beekeeping@tiscali.co.uk

DUNBLANE & STIRLING,
P. Hunt
Wildenmore, Main Street,
Gartmore FK8 3RW
01877 382594

DUNFERMLINE & WEST FIFE
J. Tout
13 Middlebank Holdings
By Dunfermline KY11 8QN
01383 415534

SBA

✉ ☎

EAST OF SCOTLAND
Mrs. H. Kinnes
Rednock, 3 Holly Road
Broughty Ferry
Dundee DD5 2LZ
01382 477762
EAST LOTHIAN, D. B. Smith
Garden Cottage
Clerkington
Haddington
East Lothian EH4 4NJ
01620 822441
gardencottage@virgin.net
EASTER ROSS
Mrs P Douglas-Menzies
Cardboll Cottage, Fearn
Ross-shire, IV20 1XP
01862 871572
EASTWOOD, R D McPhail
1 Rockmount Ave.
Thornliebank
Glasgow G46 7BU
0141 5857879
EDINBURGH & MIDLOTHIAN
P Steven
Eastercowden Cottage
Dalkeith
Midlothian
EH22 2NS
07703 528801
FIFE, Janice Furness
The Dirdale, Boarhills
St. Andrews, Fife KY16 8PP
01334 880 469
jcfurness@dirdale.fsnet.
co.uk
FORTINGALL, Mrs. Jo Pendleton,
Lilac Cottage
Old Bridge of Tilt
by Pitlochry
PH18 5TP
01796 481 362

GLASGOW DISTRICT,
Mr P Stromberg
21 Woodside Houston,
Renfrewshire
PA6 7DD
01505 613830
HELENSBURGH, M Thornley
Glenarn
Glenarn Road
Rhu, Helensburgh
G84 8LL
01436 820493
masthome@dsl.pipex.com
INVERNESS-SHIRE
Mrs S Forth
Kirkland Lodge
Wardlaw Road
Kirkhill, Inverness-shire
IV5 7NB
01463 831511
KELVIN VALLEY, I Ferguson
4 South Glassford Street
Milngavie
G62 6AT
0141 956 3963
KILBARCHAN AND DISTRICT
I. Craig
30 Burnside Ave
Brookfield
Johnstone PA5 8UT
01505 322684
KILMARNOCK & IRVINE
J. Campbell
North Kilbryde House
Stewarton
Kilmarnock KA3 3EP
01560 482489
KIRRIEMUIR, A. Bell
Valtos, Mains of Glasswell
Kirriemuir DD8 5QE
01575 572899

LARGS & DIST,
Vacant Position
LOCHABER, P.J. Browne
The Rowan Tree, Gairlochy
Spean Bridge
Inverness-shire PH34 4EQ
01397 712898
MORAY, T Harris
Cowiemuir
Fochabers
01343 821 282
MULL, Mrs. S. Barnard
Viewmount, Tobermory
Isle of Mull PA75 6PG
01688 302008
NAIRN & DISTRICT,
Ms B McLean
Upper Flat,2 Invererne Rd
Forres, IV36 1DZ
01309 676316
OBAN & DISTRICT,
Mrs Anja Lamont
Glenburn
Toberonochy
Oban, Argyll
PA34 4TY
01852 314 376
OLRIG, W. Bruce
Post Office House,
Janetstown, Thurso,
Caithness KW14 7XF
01847 892760
PEEBLES-SHIRE, G. Goldshaw
Venlaw Farm, Peebles
EH45 8QG
01721 722040
PERTHSHIRE, J. Shovlin
"Invercarse",
4 Glebe Terrace
Perth PH2 7AG
01738 627965

163

SBA

✉ ☎

SKYE & LOCHALSH, M Purrett
15 Glasnakille, Egol
Isle of Skye, IV49 9BQ
01471 866 207
S. OF SCOTLAND, A Ferguson
Firparkneuk
Kirtlebridge
Lockerbie
DG11 3LZ
01461 500322
fergiearchie@tiscali.co.uk

SUTHERLAND, Sue Steven
Mulberry Croft
2 East Newport, Berriedale
Caithness KW7 6HA
01539 751 245
WEST'N GALLOWAY, Fiona Keith
The Walled Garden
Dunragit DG9 8PH
01581 400613

WEST LINTON & DISTRICT
D. Stokes
100 Main Street, Roslin
Midlothian EH25 9LT
0131 440 3477

Freuchie BKA disbanded

SBA ACTIVE HONEY JUDGES

M BADGER
Kara,
14 Thorn Lane,
Roundhay,
Leeds LS8 1NN
MISS E. BROWN
Milton House, Main Street,
Scotlandwell
Kinross KY13 9JA
01592 840582
P.J. BROWNE
The Rowan Tree, Gairlochy
Spean Bridge
Inverness-shire PH34 4EQ
01397 712730
M. CANHAM
Whinhill Farm House
by Cawdor, Nairn IV12 5RF
01667 404314
I. CRAIG
30 Burnside Avenue
Brookfield, Johnstone
Renfrewshire, PA5 8UT
01505 322684

C. E. IRWIN
55 Lindsaybeg Road
Chryston, Glasgow
G69 9DW
0141 7791333
DR F. ISLES
"Gardenhurst",
Newbigging Broughty Ferry
Dundee DD5 3RH
01382 370315
MS B L MCLEAN
Upper Flat, 2 Invererne Rd,
Forres IV36 1DZ
01309 676316
W.B. TAYLOR
West Newbigging Cottage,
Glenbervie Road, Drumlithie
Stonehaven AB39 3YA
01569 740375
L.M. WEBSTER
Birchlea, Rothiemay, Huntly
Aberdeenshire AB54 5LN
01466 771351

C. WEIGHTMAN
Shilford, Stocksfield,
Northumberland NE43 4HW
01661 842082
C. WILSON
Cedarhill, Auchencloch,
Banknock, Bonnybridge
FK4 1VA
01324 840227
BRON WRIGHT
20 Lennox Row
Edinburgh EH3 5JW
0131 552 3439
DAVID WRIGHT
SBA General Secretary.
Sept 2009
M. YOUNG
101 Carnreagh, Hillsborough
County Down
N. Ireland BT26 6LJ
0289 268972

ULSTER BEEKEEPERS' ASSOCIATION

www.ubka.org

OBJECTS OF THE ASSOCIATION
The objects of the Association shall be to unite beekeepers for their mutual benefit to serve the best interests of beekeeping by all means within its power and to foster its healthy development.

For the purpose of achieving these objects the Association will:
• promote the formation of local Beekeepers' Associations
• disseminate information and advice about beekeeping
• provide examination facilities in the art of beekeeping
• encourage maintainenance and improvement of the beekeeping environment.

EDUCATION
In conjunction with the Department of Agriculture and Rural Development (DARD) the U.B.K.A. assists in organising classes for Preliminary, Intermediate and Senior Certificate Examinations in Beekeeping following the syllabus of the F.I.B.K.A.

INSURANCE
Affiliated local Assosiations and their individual members have access to the UBKA group public and product liability insurance scheme.

APIARY SITES
All nine affiliated local Associations and CAFRE's Greenmount Campus each have an apiary site with observation houses, provided with help from Leader 2 funding,for use in demonstrating and promoting good practice to members, schools and other interested groups

SECRETARY, David Wright
24 Quarry Road
Lisbane,Comber
Newtownards
BT23 5NF
Co Down

PRESIDENT,
Rev Margaret Johnston
45 Ballymorran Rd,
Killinchy, Newtownards
Co. Down, BT23 6UD

CHAIRMAN, Mervyn Eddie
3b Old Rd
Upper Ballinderry,Lisburn
Co. Antrim BT28 2NJ

TREASURER, Robert McCreery.
165A Ballymoney Rd
Banbridge, Co. Down
BT32 4HW

LECTURERS
Jim Fletcher
26 Coach Road, Comber
Co.Down. BT23 5QX

Ethel Irvine
24 Laraugh Ballycassidy,
Enniskillen, Co. Fermanagh.
BT94 2JT

Lorraine McBride
11, Ballyloughan Park
Ballymena, Co.Antrim,
BT43 5HW

Norman Walsh
43, Edentrillick Rd
Hillsborough, Co. Down
BT26 6PG

UBKA

Jim Fletcher
26 Coach Road, Comber
BT23 5QX
Michael Young
Mileway, Carnreagh Road
Hillsborough, Co. Down
BT26 6LJ
Norman Walsh
43 Edentrillick Rd
Hillsborough Co. Down
BT26 6NH

HONEY SHOWS

Local Associations, Horticultural and other Societies stage honey shows throughout Northern Ireland. The Northern Ireland Honey Show hosted by the Belfast City Parks Department is held annually in September in the Botanic Gardens Belfast.

CONFERENCE

The next UBKA Annual Conference will be held on 26th - 27th February 2010 at CAFRE's Greenmount Campus, Antrim. Contact the U.B.K.A. Secretary and www.ubka.org for details.

SECRETARIES OF ASSOCIATIONS

BELFAST,
David McCartney
19 Delacherois Ave,
Lisburn, Co. Antrim
BT27 4TR

DROMORE AND DISTRICT,
Vanessa Drew
40 Lacken Road
Ballyroney,
Banbridge, Co.Down
BT32 5JA

EAST ANTRIM,
Sandi McDowell
6 Gobbins Brae,
Larne, Co.Antrim
BT40 3TE

MID ANTRIM,
Lorraine McBride
11 Ballyloughlan Park
Ballymena,Co. Antrim
BT43 5HW

FERMANAGH, Brian Richardson
Agho, 305 LattoneRoad,
Belcoo, Enniskillen,
Co. Fermanagh
BT93 5ES

KILLINCHY AND DISTRICT
David McCartney
19 Delacherois Ave,
Lisburn, Co. Antrim
BT27 4TR

MID ULSTER, Ernie Watterson
Flourmill Hill, Coalisland Rd
Dungannon.
Co. Tyrone
BT71 6EP

RANDALSTOWN,
Caroline Thomson
105 Cidercourt Rd
Crumlin, Antrim,
Co. Antrim, BT29 4RX

ROE VALLEY, Billy McBride
59,SeacoastRoad,
Limavady
Co. Londonderry
BT49 9DW

CYMDEITHAS GWENYNWYR

CYMRU WELSH BEEKEEPERS' ASSOCIATION

AMCANION Y GYMDEITHAS / AIMS OF THE ASSOCIATION
- Promote and develop beekeeping in Wales
- Conduct examinations in beekeeping
- Liaise with organisations and bodies for the benefit of beekeeping in Wales

AELODAETH UNIGOL / INDIVIDUAL MEMBERSHIP
Individual membership of the WBKA is provided for persons who do not live within the areas of branch associations, and wish to support the association. Information relating to benefits and facilities provided for individual members is available from the Individual Membership Secretary.

ARHOLIADAU / EXAMINATIONS
The Examinations Board conducts six grades of examinations: Junior, Primary, Intermediate, Practical, Honey Show Judges, Senior. Information is available from the Examination Board Secretary.

Candidates following the Duke of Edinburgh Award Scheme may receive information regarding the inclusion of beekeeping as a course submission from the Examinations Secretary.

CYNHADLEDD / CONVENTION
At the Royal Welsh Agricultural Society's Showground, Llanelwedd. This event is normally held during Late March/ Early April. Information relating to this event is available from the convention secretary.

YSWIRIANT / INSURANCE
All individual and fully paid up members of beekeeping associations affiliated to WBKA are covered against 'Public and Product' liability claims. All affiliated associations are covered against public liability during conventions officially organised by the association.

YSGRIFENNYDD / SECRETARY
John Tayler
Tynewydd Cottage
Myddfai
LLandovery
01550 720473
johber@btinternet.com

LLYWYDD/PRESIDENT
Tom Rowlands
Underhill
Tyddyn To
Menai Bridge
LL59 5BL
tom@rowlands8145.
freeserve.co.uk

CADEIRYDD/CHAIR
David Culshaw
9 Ash Grove, Llay
Wrexham LL12 8LR
(01978) 854593
dcllay@aol.com

IS-GADAIRYDD/
VICE CHAIR
Mrs V Forsyth
61 High Street
Criccieth
Gwynedd LL52 0HB
01766 522 852

WBKA/CGC

✉ ☎

TRYSORYDD/TREASURER
Jim Patt
Black Lion House,Welsh St.
Bishop's Castle
SY9 5BS
01588 638828,
jim.bc@homecall.co.uk

The WBKA Individual Membership benefits include cover under the BDI Scheme against the loss, due to foul brood diseases, of a minimum number of stocks (determined by BDI). Affiliated Associations provide this cover for their members.

LLYFRGELL / LIBRARY

The reference sections of all county libraries in Wales have details of the names and addresses of Secretaries of Associations affiliated to WBKA.

Books on beekeeping can be borrowed from county, branch and mobile libraries. The Library, Ffordd y Bala, Dolgellau LL40 2YS, has been nominated to stock

GWEFEISTR/WEBMASTER
Duncan Parks
Cefn Coed, Ffordd
Graianrhyd, Llanarmon yn lal
Yr Wyddgrug CH7 4QW
(01824) 780504
duncan@the-parks.com

beekeeping books.

Members of associations affiliated to IBRA may borrow books/documents from its library.

GWENYNWYR CYMRU - The Welsh Beekeeper

A publication of the Welsh Beekeepers Association, giving news and views of beekeeping and related subjects. Articles and advertisements enquiries should be sent to the Editor. Articles written in Welsh should be sent to the Sub Editor. Gwenynwyr Cymru is provided free to members of Affiliated Associations and Individual Members. Information regarding subscriptions is available from the Individual Membership / Subscription Secretary.

IS-OLYGYDD (ERTHYGLAU CYMRAEG)/SUB EDITOR
Dewi Morris Jones
Llwynderw, Bronant
Aberystwyth SY23 4TG
(01974 251264)

GOLYGYDD/EDITOR
Mr P Rand
Dayleen,Pontsian
Llandysul, SA44 4UB
01545590313

GWASANAETH CLYWELED / AUDIO-VISUAL AIDS SERVICE

This service is available to all affiliated associations and individual members. Further information is available from the Audio-Visual Aids Secretary.

DARLITHWYR / DANGOSWYR, LECTURERS / DEMONSTRATORS

The names and addresses of lecturers and demonstrators, recommended by associations affiliated to the WBKA, are available from the General Secretary.

ARHOLIADAU/EXAMINATIONS
D.H. Ferguson Thomas
Erw Lon, Llanwrda SA19 8HD
(01550) 777132

CYNLLUN CYSWLLT CHWYSTRELLU / SPRAY LIAISON SCHEME

Information is available from the General secretary

✉ ☎

SIOEAU / SHOWS

Honey/beekeeping sections are included at the Royal Welsh Agricultural Show, Llanelwedd, (OS ref: SO040520) during July, and at county, town and village shows throughout Wales. Information relating to these events may be obtained from secretaries of associations in the locality of the shows.

The historic FFAIR FEL ABERCONWY is held annually in the main street of the town, (OS ref: SH278378), on 13th September. Further information is available from the secretary of Conwy Association.

RHEOLAU CYFREITHIOL / STATUTORY REGULATIONS

The administration of the statutory regulations governing all aspects of beekeeping in Wales, is the responsibility of the Wales National Assembly, Caerdydd, CF99 1NA Phone (02920) 825111 Fax: (02920) 823352 Matters concerning statutory regulations, their implications and execution, should be addressed to the Minister of Agriculture and Rural Affairs, Wales National Assembly, at the above address.

AELODAETH UNIGOL-TANYSGRIFAU/ INDIVIDUAL MEMBERSHIP SUBSCRIPTIONS

Jane Frank
61 Fir Court Ave
Churchstoke
Montgomery, Powys
SY15 6BA
01588 620711
janefrank@bluebottle.com

YSWIRIANT/INSURANCE
CONTACT TREASURER FOR INFORMATION

CYMHORTHAU CLYWELED/ AUDIO-VISUAL AIDS

F. G. Eckton
Cartref, Llanafan Fawr
Llanfair Ym Muallt LD2 3LT
01591 620456

YSGRIFENNYDD CYMANFA/ CONVENTION SECRETARY

T. J. Rowlands
Underhill, Tyddyn To
Porth Aethwy, Ynys Mon
LL59 5BL
01248 712652

YSGRIFENNYDD STONDINAU CYMANFACONVENTION TRADE STANDS SECRETARY

M. W. Shaw, Llwyn Ysgaw
Dwyran, Llanfairpwll, Ynys Mon LL 61 6RH
01248 430811

WBKA/CGC

✉ ☎

CYMDEITHASAU TADOGOL A'U YSGRIFENYDDION / AFFILIATED ASSOCIATIONS AND SECRETARIES

ABERYSTWYTH, Ann Ovens
Tan-y-Cae
Nr. Talybont, Ceredigion
SY24 5OL
01970 832359
YNYS MON/ANGLESEY
Wally Shaw
Llwyn Ysgaw, Dwyran
Llanfairpwll, Ynys Môn
LL61 6RH
01248 430811
jenny.shaw@homecall.co.uk
BRYCHEINIOG A MAESYFED/
BRECKNOCK & RADNOR
Dr G Todd
Meadow Breeze, Llandew
Brecon
LD3 9SP
01874 610902
gbtodd@btinternet.com
PENYBONT A'R CYLCH/
BRIDGEND & DISTRICT
Mrs. S E Verran
Ty Mel,Maesteg Rd
Bridgend,CF32 oEE
01656 729699
Verran@btinternet.com
CAERDYDD A'R FRO/CARDIFF &
THE VALE
Barbara Chick
11 Porthcawl Road,
Ely, Cardiff CF5 5HU
02920 597275
barbara@beechick.
fsnet.co.uk

CAERFYRDDIN/
CARMARTHENSHIRE
Mr Brian Jones
Cwmburry Honey Farm,
Ferryside, Carmarthenshire
SA17 5TW
01267 267318
beegeejay2003@yahoo.
co.uk
CONWY,
P. McFadden
Ynys Goch, Ty'n y Groes
Conwy LL32 8UH
01492 650851
peter@honeyfair.
freeserve.co.uk
DWYRAIN CAERFYRDDIN /EAST
CAMARTHEN, John Tayler
Tynewydd Cottage
Myddfai, Llandovery
SA20 0QD
01550 720473
johber@btinternet.com
FFLINT A'R CYLCH/FLINT &
DISTRICT,
Jill & Graham Wheeler
Mertyn Downing
Whitford, Nr Holywell
Flintshire CH8 9EP
mertyndowning@
btinternet.com
GWENYNWYR CYMRAEG
CEREDIGION,
W.I. Griffiths
Llaindeg, Comins Coch
Aberystwyth SY23 3BG
01970 623334
william_griffiths05@
tiscali.co.uk

LLANBED A'R CYLCH/LAMPETER
& DISTRICT
Gordon Lumby
Gwynfryn, Brynteg
Llanybydder SA40 9UX
01570 480571
g.lumby@btopenworld.com
LLYN AC EIFIONYDD
Mrs Valerie Forsyth
61, High Street, Cricieth
Gwynedd, LL52 0HB
01766 522852
llynae@wbka.com
MEIRIONYDD, Lesley Bay
Hen Orsaf, Gellilydan
Blaenau Ffestiniog
LL41 4EP
01766 590488
bazurka@aol.com
TREFALDWYN/MONTGOMERY
Jessica Bennet
Plasheulwen, Llanfair Road
Newton, Powys, SY16 3JY
01686 626872
jessica.bennet@virgin.net
SIR BENFRO /PEMBROKESHIRE
Mr J Dudman
Sevenoaks, The Kilns
Llangwm, Haverfordwest,
Pembrokeshire, SA62 4HG
01437 891892
secretarypbka@hotmal.com
DE CLWYD/SOUTH CLWYD
Mrs Beryl Reynolds
Glandwr, Corwen, LL21 0HN
01490 412163
scbeekeepers@tiscali.co.uk

Abertawe a'r Cylch/Swansea &
District, Paul Lyons
2 West Cliff, Southgate
Swansea, SA3 2AN
paullyons@btinternet.com
GLANNAU TEIFI/TEIFISIDE
Mr John Page
The Old Tannery
Pontsian, LLandysul
Ceredigion SA44 4UD
01545 590515

GORLLEWIN MORGANNWG/WEST
GLAMORGAN
Mr John Beynon
48, Whitestone Avenue
Bishopston
Swansea SA3 3DA
jakbeynon@btinternet.com

*HEB DADOGU/NON
AFFILIATED:*
Mrs J Bromley
Ty Hir, Monmouth Road
Raglan, Usk. NP15 2ET
01291 690331
bromleyjan@hotmail.com

BEIRNIAID SIOE FÊL TRWYDDEDIG / WBKA QUALIFIED HONEY SHOW

TERRY E ASHLEY
Meadow Cottage
11 Elton Lane, Winterley
Sandbach CW11 4TN
M. BESSENT
Gwili Lodge
Heol Lot Wen, Rhydaman
SA18 3RP
ROBERT BREWER
Georgia, USA

L. CHIRNSIDE
Bryn Y Pant Cottage
Llanofer, Y Fenni
NP7 9ES
IFOR C EDWARDS   Lleifior
Pont rhyd y Groes
Ystrad Meurig SY25 6ND
G.J. HARTSHORN
31 Victoria Road
Croesoswallt SY11 2HT
MRS. D. SWEET GRAIG
Fawr Lodge, Caerffili
CF83 1NF

H. TAYLOR
14 Pentle Drive
Pentlepoir, Saundersfoot
SA69 9BW
D.H. FERGUSON THOMAS
Erw Lon, Llanwrda
SA19 8HD
REDMOND WILLIAMS
Tincurry, CAHIR, Co
Tipperary, Eire
MICHAEL YOUNG
Mileaway, Carnreagh
Hillsborough, BT26 6LJ

**THE.NATIONAL
HONEY.SHOW**

www.honeyshow.co.uk
THE 2010 SHOW IS
AT ST GEORGE'S COLLEGE,
WEYBRIDGE
28TH - 30TH OCTOBER

CSL

⊠ ☎

CENTRAL SCIENCE LABORATORY
NATIONAL BEE UNIT

www.csl.gov.uk.co.uk

02GA10
Central Science Laboratory
National Bee Unit
02F10
Sand Hutton
YORK
YO41 1LZ

Tel.No: 01904 462510
Fax.No: 01904 462240
E-Mail: nbu@csl.gov.uk
Website:
http://beebase.csl.gov.uk
www.csl.gov.uk.co.uk
Policy :   www.defra.gov.uk

NATIONAL BEE UNIT IS NOW UNDER THE FOOD AND ENVIRONMENT RESEARCH AGENCY (FERA)

THE CSL NATIONAL BEE UNIT

The National Bee Unit (NBU) is part of the Central Science Laboratory, an executive agency of the Department for Environment, Food and Rural Affairs (Defra), and is located based just outside York. The Unit is an element of CSL's Plant Health Group (PHG) and its work covers all aspects of bee health and husbandry in England and Wales, on behalf of Defra in England and for the Welsh Assembly Government DEPC in Wales (Department for Environment, Planning and the Countryside). The work of the unit includes disease and pest diagnosis, research into bee health matters, development of contingency plans for emerging threats, import risk analysis, related extension work and consultancy services to both government and industry.

NATIONAL BEE UNIT TECHNICAL
STAFF, HEAD OF UNIT
Mike Brown

HOME BASED STAFF:

NATIONAL BEE INSPECTOR
Mr R Ball
01395 567990
07855 543901

BEE HEALTH INSPECTION SERVICE

The Integrated Bee Health Programme is run by the NBU on behalf of core policy customers. The NBU has a long track record in bee husbandry and bee disease control (since 1946) and has been directly responsible for the bee inspection services in England and Wales since 1994.

The NBU consists of a home-based inspectorate team, and the laboratory diagnostic and research team based at CSL, York. In addition colleagues across CSL contribute to the programme and research projects.

The Bee Health Inspectorate

The inspectorate team consists of approximately 45 home-based members of staff. It is headed by the National Bee Inspector (NBI, whose role it is to run the statutory disease control and training programmes. The NBI has management responsibility for eight home-based Regional Bee Inspectors (RBIs), one heading each of the seven regions in England and one covering Wales. The RBI in turn manages a number of experienced Seasonal Bee Inspectors (SBIs). The RBIs and SBIs in England organise inspections under EU and UK legislation, submit suspect samples for diagnosis, treat colonies for foul brood and train beekeepers in bee husbandry for better disease control and greater self-sufficiency. In addition the bee inspectors also collect honey samples for residue analysis under the Statutory Honey collection agreement with Defra Veterinary Medicines Directorate (VMD). With Aethina tumida (small hive beetle (SHB)) and Tropilaelaps spp. now being notifiable under UK and EU law inspectors also undertake surveillance for these exotics in "at risk apiaries" close to ports of entry for example.

BEE DISEASE DIAGNOSTIC TEAM

The NBU's diagnostic team provides a rapid, modern diagnostic service for both the inspection service and beekeepers. The NBU laboratory is Good Laboratory Practice (GLP) compliant, a quality accreditation scheme administered by the Department of Health. All diagnostic tests are conducted according to the OIE (Office International des Epizooties) Manual of Standard Diagnostic Tests and Vaccines. The OIE is the world organisation for animal health and produce internationally recognised disease diagnosis guidelines (http//www.oie.int.) Across CSL diagnostic support is provided from teams of microbiologists acarologists, insect virologists and molecular specialists in the CSL Molecular Technology Unit (MTU).

BEES AND THE LAW

The Bees Act 1980 UK empowers Agriculture Ministers to make Orders to control pests and diseases affecting bees, and provides powers of entry for authorised persons. Under the Bees Act, The Bee Diseases and Pests Control Order 2006 for England and Wales, (there is similar legislation for Scotland and Northern Ireland)

REGIONAL BEE INSPECTORS
Mr I Molyneux
(Northern Region)
01204 381186
07815 872604
Mr D Sutton (Western Region)
01885 483136
07813 510676
Mr I Homer (Southern Region)
01308 482161
07778 846335
Mr A Byham (South East Region)
01306 611016
07890 831327
Mr A Vevers (South West Region)
01364 653325
07977 336574
Mr A Wattam (Eastern Region)
01522 789726
07791 085207
Mr I Flatman
(N'th Eastern Region)
01924 257089
Mr J Verran (Wales)
01656 729669
07855 543851

FOR DETAILS OF SEASONAL BEE INSPECTORS DETAILS CONTACT THE RELEVANT RBI OR CHECK BEEBASE

CSL

✉ ☎

LABORATORY BASED STAFF
Research Co-ordinator
Giles Budge

Laboratory & Apiary Manager
Selwyn Wilkins

LABORATORY TECHNICAL STAFF
Ben Jones

ADMINISTRATIVE OFFICERS
Office Administrator
Kate Parker

Assistant administrator
Vacancy

designates American foulbrood (AFB), European foulbrood (EFB), A. tumida (SHB) and Tropilaelaps mites (all species) as notifiable pests and defines the action which may be taken in the event of outbreaks.

At the European level, the Directive on animal health requirements for trade in bees is called the Balai Directive (92/65/EEC) implemented in the UK under the Animal and Animal Products (Import and Export) Regulations. It lists American foul brood (AFB), the small hive beetle (A. tumida) and Tropilaelaps mites as notifiable pests and diseases throughout the EU (at the time of writing time neither the small hive beetle nor Tropilaelaps have been confirmed in Europe).

THE IMPORTATION OF BEES

It is legal to import Queen bees from third countries, the rules governing this are set out in Commission Decision 2003/881/EC, as amended by Commission Decision 2005/60/EC. The list of countries is currently restricted to, Argentina, Australia, Hawaii and New Zealand.

It is legal to import bees freely from the EU (including queens, packages and colonies). Under the Balai directive consignments of bees moved between Member States must be accompanied by an original health certificate confirming freedom from notifiable pests and diseases.

For full details on the importation of bees from within the EU or from Third countries please either consult the Defra website (http://www.defra.gov.uk/hort/Bees/index.htm) or contact the NBU.

AMERICAN AND EUROPEAN FOUL BROOD

Foul brood-infected apiaries are placed under standstill notice, supervised by the bee inspector, until the disease is cleared from the apiary and the honey from antibiotic-treated colonies is safe to harvest. We always aim to minimise the impact of this as far as possible, in co-operation with the beekeeper.

VARROA

As part of the NBU's routine field screening programme the first known case of resistant varroa mites in the

UK was discovered in apiaries in Devon in August 2001. The NBU undertook a resistance-monitoring programme throughout England and Wales. Varroa resistant mites are now widespread in England and Wales. To see the current status of the resistance of varroa mites to pyrethroids and the latest advice on treatments please visit the NBU website (http://beebase.csl.gov.uk/).

ADULT BEE DISEASES
The NBU also look for adult bee diseases and parasites such as Nosema species (*Nosema apis* and *osema. ceranae*, amoeba (*Malpighamoeba mellificae*) and tracheal mites (*Acarine* or *Acarapis woodi*) from samples submitted by beekeepers. As these diseases are non-statutory this service is chargeable. For the current cost please contact the NBU. Bees that have been imported from designated Third countries are also checked for disease and are also screened for exotic pests potentially harmful to UK beekeeping.

EXOTICS
Beekeepers must make themselves aware of the potential threats to beekeeping in the UK. The field inspection team monitors for potential exotics, the SHB and Tropilaelaps spp. The laboratory team also routinely screen import samples and suspect samples submitted for identification by both beekeepers and the field team.

PESTICIDE MONITORING
The Wildlife Incident Investigation Scheme (WIIS) is a unique Defra scheme for monitoring the effects of pesticides on wildlife, including honey bees, and is used as a model by other countries. Samples of bees from a suspected spray poisoning incident are sent to the NBU are screened for disease prior to residue analysis by the Wildlife Incident Unit. Reports from incidents are used by the independent Environmental Panel (which reports to the Advisory Committee on Pesticides) to identify and solve any problems with the use of misuse of agrochemicals, wherever possible.

RESEARCH & DEVELOPMENT
A programme of research and development within the group underpins the Unit's work. They also have long-established

links with many European and world wide research centres, beekeeping specialists and beekeepers to ensure we keep up to date with current beekeeping trends and research. Some of the most recent projects have included the development of rapid diagnostics techniques for foulbrood and viruses. Lateral flow diagnostic kits (the development of which was funded by Vita Europe Ltd) are now used routinely in the UK for the field diagnosis of AFB and EFB. There has also been the development and introduction of the Shook Swarm treatment method for EFB, which the NBU has been investigating for the past several years. We are currently working on a 'one-stop shop' for bee disease diagnosis using molecular biology techniques. The primary aim of our R & D is to provide up-to-date technical support to beekeepers and to our Bee Health Inspection Service. Also the NBU has three PhD students studying various topics including the discrimination of AFB bacteria, the taxonomy of UK honey bee viruses and the characterisation and distribution of bee diseases and parasites in Thailand. For an update on R&D work at the unit see the NBU website.

The main areas of R&D are foul brood, Varroa, exotics, viruses and the impact of agriculture on bees.

RISK ASSESSMENT

The National Bee Unit manages 150 honeybee colonies and has much experience in assessing the effects and efficacy of veterinary bee medicines (e.g., varroacides) and pesticides in both field and laboratory tests. Our Good Laboratory Practice (GLP) accreditation allows us to undertake a wide range of routine and specially designed laboratory, semi-field and field studies on honeybees and bumblebees for regulatory authorities and industry worldwide.

EXTENSION

The NBU helps train beekeepers in several ways: local courses and advisory visits run by the inspectors, and national courses held at the York laboratory. Over the past seven years the NBU has hosted National Diploma in Beekeeping residential courses and has also been host to visiting overseas workers and researchers. NBU

York based staff also provide training to beekeepers at local and regional beekeeper meetings.

THE BEE HEALTH ADVISORY PANEL

This CSL panel includes representatives from the BBKA, WBKA, BFA, CONBA, and BDI. It also has independent members from the bee industry. Formed in 1999, the panel monitors the CSL National Bee Unit performance against agreed standards, but more importantly it influences modernisation of procedures under the Bees Act to cope with changes affecting industry And helps the NBU with improving the service provided for beekeepers

BEEBASE ONLINE

BeeBase is a web-based data base acting as an Information Warehouse. Originally funded by the Defra Challenge Fund, work began on this project in 2005. The database was developed the Knowledge management group (part of CSL) on behalf of the NBU. For the first time it allows Beekeepers to access their own apiary records, diagnostic histories and details over the web.

Beekeepers can register online as a Beekeeper and can request an apiary visit from their local inspector who will provide any help and advice needed. The website also provides information on the functional activities of the NBU, legislation, pests and diseases including their recognition and control, interactive maps, current research areas, publications, advisory leaflets and key contacts.

DARD/NI

✉ ☎

DEPARTMENT OF AGRICULTURE AND RURAL DEVELOPMENT FOR NORTHERN IRELAND

www.dardni.gov.uk

BEE ADVISER FOR THE DEPARTMENT
Paul Moore
Agriculture & Food Science Centre Newforge Lane
BELFAST BT9 5PX
028 9025 5288
Fax: 028 9025 5003
E-mail, Paul.J.Moore@ dardni.gov.uk

TRAINING COURSES:
Greenmount Campus
College of Agriculture Food and Rural Enterprise:
INFORMATION IS AVAILABLE FROM THE COLLEGE AT
028 9442 6631
Fax: 028 9442 6606
E-mail, Kevin.O'Donnell@ dardni.gov.uk

Honeybee Regional Report for Northern Ireland 2007

Bee Health Surveys

Speculation in the media of the threat of CCD to local bees ensured that the Bee Inspectorate had to deal with increased reports of bee losses in the spring. While there is no doubt that bee associations could point to high losses amongst beekeepers often it seemed to be the case that varroa monitoring and control could be greatly improved. Findings of high levels of varroa mites in some of the samples lifted in the autumn for varroacide resistance testing would indicate that this remains the case.

The Bee Inspectorate carried out surveys for American foul brood, European foul brood, Small Hive beetle and Tropilaelaps mite along with sampling of bees for resistance testing of varroa mites. American foul brood outbreaks remained high with twelve apiaries found to have the disease. The outbreaks were in many new areas this year indicating a widespread disease presence. No cases of European foul brood were recorded although a number of hives were checked using the field test kits and laboratory analysis. Surveys continued for Small Hive Beetle and Tropilaelaps mite. Apiaries in the vicinity of ports or fruit importers were targeted for Small Hive Beetle inspections using corriboard shelter traps while apiaries that had imported in the past were selected and hive scrapings examined for Tropilaelaps mite.

Varroa

Submissions have reduced significantly since last year as all of the associations reported positive infestation in their areas. As varroa mite incidence has reached a complete establishment within Northern Ireland, more emphasis was

178

placed on advice on treatment applications and associated resistance monitoring. As in 2006, monitoring was directed at areas of early varroa establishment. Two previous apiaries displaying resistance to treatment had their colonies replaced and no indication of varroacide resistance was recorded.

Again this year more associations are investigating alternative varroa treatments as part of a pest management strategy.

Adult Bee Disease Diagnostics
Acarine and Nosema are both still in evidence although only low numbers of samples were received this year. Concern perhaps was directed to the overall loss of bees and no bodies to submit for analysis.

Residue Sampling
Honey samples were again lifted this year for testing for residues of veterinary medicines and environmental contaminants. Samples lifted last year were found to be satisfactory.

Imports
Thirty-one imports were notified to DARD and a number of follow-up inspections were carried out to check the records and health certificates. These imports came from Greece and Denmark. In some cases health certificates aren't accompanying bees and also notification by beekeepers isn't being carried out. One such incident was raised with the relevant authorities.

**The Bee Diseases and Pests Control Order
(Northern Ireland) 2007**
The above Order came into operation on the 21st May 2007, which brought our list of notifiable pests and diseases into line with England and Wales. Work has started on the Bee Health contingency plan and it is hoped to have a draft of this ready to go to the various bee organisations in February 2008 for consultation.

Thomas Williamson
Senior Bee Inspector DARD
Paul Moore
Bee Disease Diagnostics AFBI
Seamus Hughes
Farm Policy Branch, DARD

SASA

SCOTTISH AGRICULTURAL SCIENCE AGENCY

THE SCOTTISH EXECUTIVE ENVIRONMENT AND RURAL AFFAIRS DEPARTMENT

HEADQUARTERS
Pentland House
FAO Neil Henderson
Room 313, 47 Robbs Loan
Edinburgh EH14 1TY
(0131) 244 633096
e-mail, animal.heath@
scotland.gsi.gov.uk

The Scottish Government Rural Payments and Inspections Directorate (SGRPID) has responsibility for policy matters, the control of the movement of bees in the event of an outbreak of a statutory notifiable disease, maintaining records of disease incidents, issuing import licences for queen bees, initiating enforcement action where bee mortalities have resulted from the misuse or abuse of pesticides and for liaison with the Scottish Beekeepers Association.

EXECUTIVE AGENCY, SCOTTISH AGRICULTURAL SCIENCE AGENCY
1 Roddinglaw Rd, Edinburgh
EH12 9FJ

BEE DISEASES, Jane Chard
Plant Health Section
(0131) 244 8863
PESTICIDE INCIDENTS,
Elizabeth Sharp
Chemistry Section
(0131) 244 8874

SGRPID

Agricultural Officers, located at area offices throughout Scotland, carry out field inspections following notification of bee mortalities resulting from the misuse of pesticides. Bees Officers investigate notified incidents of statutory bee diseases.

The Scottish Agricultural Science Agency (SASA) has responsibility for the analysis of pesticides in dead bees and diagnosis of statutory bee diseases.

BEE DISEASES

Under the Bee Diseases Control Order 1982, beekeepers are required to notify SGRPID of suspected cases of foul brood diseases or varroasis. These should be notifed to the Principal Agricultural Officer (PAO) at the nearest SGRPID Area Office who will arrange for a Bees Officer to carry out an inspection. Brood combs or hive debris from colonies thought to be infected will be sent to SASA for laboratory examination. Alternatively, a beekeeper may send hive debris direct to Plant Health Section, (Bee Diseases), SASA, at the above address for examination for the parasitic mite, Varroa destructor.

Following the detection of varroa in Devon in April 1992, widespread searches of bee colonies have been carried out in autumn in Great Britain to assess the spread of the disease. The areas of England, Wales ,mainland Scotland and the island of Bute have been declared as Statutory Infected Areas (SIAs) and the movement of bees from these areas is prohibited. To help prevent the spread of infection into Scotland, only Queen Bees with attendant workers may be moved, under licence, into Scotland under both the Importation of Bees Order 1980 (from outwith Great Britain) and the Bee Diseases Control Order 1982 (from the SIAs). Queen Bees are inspected by SGRPID Bees Officers at the premises of the importer and attendant workers are sent to SASA for examination for the presence of varroa. **No charge is made for this service.**

PESTICIDE INCIDENTS

As part of the Wildlife Incident Investigation Scheme, SASA undertakes analytical investigations into bee mortalities where pesticide poisoning may have been involved. Beekeepers should send samples of dead bees (200) direct to SASA, Chemistry Section, for analysis. In the case of major incidents, beekeepers are advised to contact the PAO at the nearest Area Office so that an early field investigation can be instigated. A report will be issued to the beekeeper and if appropriate, enforcement action under the Control of Pesticides Regulations 1986 will be initiated. **No charges are made for these services.**

SGRPID

✉ ☎

THE SCOTTISH GOVERNMENT RURAL PAYMENTS AND INSPECTIONS DIRECTORATE BEE INSPECTORS

THE FOLLOWING SCOTTISH GOVERNMENT RURAL PAYMENTS AND INSPECTIONS DIRECTORATE (SGRPID) STAFF ARE AUTHORISED BEE INSPECTORS.

ANGUS/N.E. FIFE,PERTH AREA OFFICE, Sandy Lister/
Paul Svenson
Strathern House,
Broxden Business Park,
Lamberkine Drive, Perth,
Perth & Kinross, PH1 1RZ
(01738 602000
Fax: (01738) 602001
ARGYLL & WESTERN ISLES OBAN AREA OFFICE
Steve Sunderland
Cameron House,
Albany Street, Oban
PA34 4AE
(01631) 563071
Fax: (01631) 566756
GRAMPIAN - INVERURIE AREA OFFICE,
Kirsteen Sutherland
Thainstone Court,
Inverurie, Grampian,
Aberdeenshire, AB51 5YA
(01467) 626247
Fax: (01467) 626217

HIGHLAND - INVERNESS AREA, OFFICE:
Clem Cuthbert
Longman House,
 28 Longman Road,
Inverness IV1 1SF
(01463) 253053
Fax: (01463) 714697
NORTHERN - THURSO AREA OFFICE:
Murdo Mackenzie
Strathbeg House,
 Clarence Street,
Thurso KW14 7JS
(01847) 893104
Fax: (01847) 895983
NORTHERN ISLES - KIRKWALL AREA, OFFICE:
Niel McCarthy
Tankerness Lane, Kirkwall,
Orkney KW15 1AQ
(01856) 875444
Fax: (01856) 873309

SOUTHERN - DUMFRIES AREA OFFICE,
Angus Cameron
161 Brooms Road, Dumfries
DG1 3ES
(01387) 274400
Fax: (01387) 274440
SOUTH EASTERN - GALASHIELS AREA OFFICE,
Angus MacAskill
Cotgreen Road,
Tweedbank, Galashiels,
Scottish Borders, TD1 3SG
(01896) 892400
Fax: (01896) 892424
SOUTH WESTERN - AYR AREA OFFICE,
John Smith
Russell House, King Street,
Ayr, South Ayrshire,
KA8 0BG
(01292) 291300
Fax: (01292) 611483
HAMILTON - SUB OFFICE
Brian Lindsay Cadzow Court, 3
Wellhall Road,Hamilton
ML3 9BG
(01698) 281166
Fax: (01698) 285277

WWW.SCOTLAND.GOV.UK/TOPICS/APICULTURE/GRANTS/INSPECTIONS/BEEINSPECTIONS

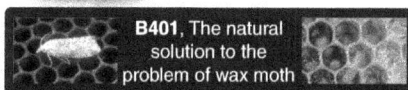

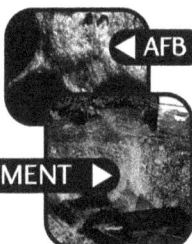

USEFUL TABLES

BEEKEEPING METRIC CONVERTION TABLES

°CENT	FAHR	INCH	MM	INCH	MM	INCH	MM
0	32	$1/25$	1	$1^5/8$	42	10	254
5	40	$1/12$	2	$1^{11}/16$	43	$10^1/4$	260
7	44	$1/8$	3	$1^9/20$	48	$11^1/4$	286
30	86	$1/16$	5	2	51	$11^1/2$	292
34	92	$1/4$	6	3	76	$11^3/4$	298
38	100	$5/16$	8	$4^1/4$	108	12	305
43	110	$3/8$	9	$4^1/2$	114	14	356
49	120	$1/2$	12.5	$4^3/4$	121	$16^1/4$	413
54	130	$5/8$	16	$5^1/2$	140	$16^1/2$	49
60	140	$3/4$	18	$5^3/4$	146	17	431
62	144	$7/8$	22	6	152	$17^5/8$	448
82	180	1	25	$6^1/4$	159	$18^1/8$	460
90	194	$1^1/16$	27	$8^1/4$	216	$18^1/4$	483
100	212	$1^3/8$	35	$8^3/4$	223	20	508
		$1^9/20$	37	$9^1/8$	232	$21^1/2$	546
		$1^1/2$	38	$9^3/8$	239	$21^3/4$	552
				$9^9/16$	246	22	559

INTERNATIONAL QUEEN MARKING COLOURS

YEAR ENDING	COLOUR	REMEMBER
1 & 6	WHITE	Will
2 & 7	YELLOW	You
3 & 8	RED	Raise
4 & 9	GREEN	Good
5 & 0	BLUE	Bees?

BOTTOM BEE-SPACE HIVES

No, of cells in brood box
Lug length (MM)
Frame spacing (mm)
Frame size (mm)
No. frames
Hive tvpe

Hive type		No. frames	Frame size (mm)	Frame spacing (mm)	Lug length (MM)	No. of cells in brood box
National	BROOD	11	356 x 216	37	38	58000
	SUPER	10	356 x 140	42	38	36000
Modified Commercial	BROOD	11	406 x 254	37	16	75000
	SUPER	10	406 x 152	42	16	

TOP BEE-SPACE HIVES

No, of cells in brood box
Lug length (MM)
Frame spacing (mm)
Frame size (mm)
No. frames
Hive tvpe

Hive type		No. frames	Frame size (mm)	Frame spacing (mm)	Lug length (MM)	No. of cells in brood box
Smith	BROOD	11	356 x 216	37	18	58000
	SUPER	10	356 x 140	42	18	36000
Langstroth	BROOD	10	448 x 232	35	16	68000
	SUPER	10	448 x 140	35	16	
Jumbo	BROOD	10	448 x 286	35	16	85000
	SUPER	10	448 x 140	35	16	
Modified Dadant	BROOD	11	448 x 286	37	16	93000
	SUPER	10	448 x 159	42	16	

USEFUL TABLES

CONVERSION FACTORS

TEMPERATURE

Fahrenheit > Celcius (Centigrade)	- 32, x 0.5555 ($^5/_9$)
Celcius > Fahrenheit	x 1.8 ($^9/_5$), + 32

WEIGHT

Ounces > Pounds	x 28.3495
Pounds > Grams	x 453.59237
Hundredweights > Kilograms	x 50.8
Grams > Ounces	'/. 28.3495
Kilograms > Pounds	x 2.2142

LENGTH

Inches > Centimetres	x 2.54
Yards > Metres	x 0.9144
Miles > Kilometres	x 1.609
Centimetres > Inches	x 0.3937
Metres > Yards	x 1.0936
Kilometres > Miles	'/. 1.609

AREA

Acres > Hectares	x 0.404686
Hectares > Acres	x 2.47105

VOLUMN

Pints > Litres	x 0.5683
Gallons > Litres	x 4.546
Litres > Pints	x 1.7598
Litres > Gallons	x 0.21997

✉ ☎